To Dad/Grandpa/Alan –

P A R I S
THE CITY AND ITS PHOTOGRAPHERS

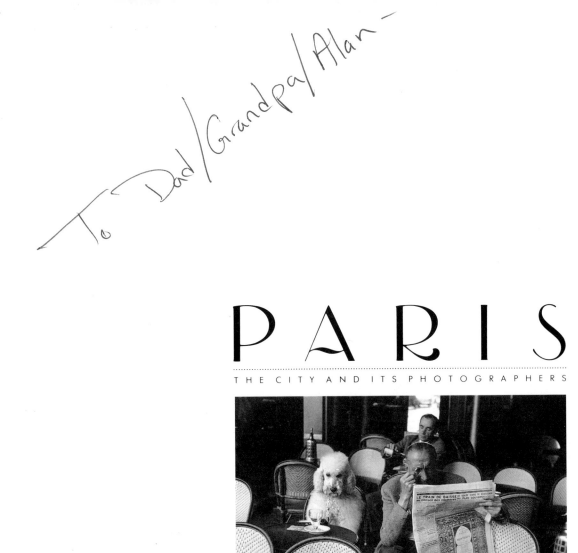

Father's Day 1996

Enjoy your first fathers day as a

Grand-father –

Love – Emilie, Jim, and

Nicholas

PARIS

THE CITY AND ITS PHOTOGRAPHERS

PATRICK DEEDES-VINCKE

A Bulfinch Press Book
Little, Brown and Company
Boston Toronto London

For Lucy and Lola

Copyright © 1992 by Patrick Deedes-Vincke

Photographic acknowledgements appear on page 141

First Edition

ISBN (Britain) 0-316-88892-3
CIP data for this book is available from the British Library.

ISBN (North America) 0-8212-1962-6
Library of Congress Catalog Card Number 91-59005
Library of Congress Cataloging-in-Publication information is available.

Designed by Andrew Barron and Collis Clements Associates
Typeset by Florencetype Ltd, Kewstoke, Avon, UK
Duotone separations by Fotographics, Hong Kong

Published simultaneously in the United States of America by
Bulfinch Press, an imprint and trademark of Little, Brown and Company (Inc.),
in Great Britain by Little, Brown and Company (UK) Ltd,
and in Canada by Little, Brown & Company (Canada) Limited

PRINTED IN ITALY

Half-title page: *Saint Germain des Près*, Boubat 1951
Facing title page: *Rue Rotrou, View of an Arcade at the Odéon*, Ilse Bing 1952
Title page: *Steps in Montmartre*, Brassaï *c.*1935

CONTENTS

A poem by Ady
Kertész 1927–8

PREFACE

Photography, since its beginnings in Paris in the first half of the last century, has contributed immeasurably to our appreciation of the city's beauty and understanding of its history. If our collective vision of Paris is one of romance, of the Seine and its bridges, of the parks and their lovers, and of rooftop views through garret windows, this too is due largely to the art which most memorably captures the city's nobility and serenity – an art which the city quickly claimed as its own.

The relationship which has grown up between Paris and photography is an extraordinary one. Photography allows us the privilege of observing the detail and emotion of a fleeting instant, capturing its subject for a moment that would otherwise be lost for ever. When that subject is Paris in its many different guises, the result is a heady mixture of 'an impression of reality with the fantasy of dreams', as photography was described by early critics. It was not until I was commissioned to write this book, however, that I became aware of the vast richness of the legacy left to us by the 'Magicians of Light'. The archives I consulted turned out to be a veritable Pandora's box, as one photograph led to another, each one as worthy of inclusion as the next. The decision to go no further than 1968 was deliberate, for with the student riots of that year and the ensuing disruption, and with the urban upheaval of the mid-1960s, came the end of an era; our collective memory of the city was set firmly in the past with some degree of nostalgia. The many different disciplines and styles that have proliferated since then deserve a book of their own. The images I have chosen, I hope, belong to that secret drawer of our imagination and of our dreams. They remain, by necessity, a personal choice, but I hope they go some way towards being a fitting testimony to both the magnificence of each photographer's vision and the timeless beauty of the city of Paris.

Patrick Deedes-Vincke

Rue du Plâtre
Marville *c.*1858

THE INVENTION OF PHOTOGRAPHY & ITS GOLDEN AGE

1839 ▶ 1888

The organ-grinder from Barbarie
Nègre 1853

On 19 August 1839, an unusually large crowd gathered in the public gallery of the Institut de France for a joint sitting of the Académie des Sciences and the Académie des Beaux Arts. They had come to listen to the public announcement of the invention of the 'daguerreotype', a process which was being much talked about in scientific and artistic circles in Paris. Some would have been keen to hear the exact details of the process as it was described by Count François Arago during the session, hoping to try it for themselves; others may simply have had a passing interest in man's new-found ability to capture 'the imprint of nature'. Few, however, would have been aware of the extent to which Daguerre's invention would change our perception of the world.

Louis-Jacques Mandé Daguerre was the inventor of a highly sophisticated form of theatrical scenery known as the Diorama. Situated in the fashionable district of the Faubourg du Temple, the Diorama drew people from all over France. A celebrated painter and theatre decorator by trade, Daguerre was able, through an ingenious system of lights projected on to large-scale paintings of rural scenes and sumptuous interiors, to bring an element of reality to the changing sequence of panels. He very quickly made a name for himself, and a visit to the Diorama was soon being highly recommended in *The Foreigner's Guide to Paris*, the city's guidebook of the day.

Although it is now known that photography was born out of several simultaneous and complementary innovations in the fields of optical science and chemistry, the announcement of the daguerreotype was the first time that such a development was brought to the attention of the outside world. The effect was remarkable. Within a few days opticians were flooded with orders for the necessary equipment; by 2 September Daguerre was giving classes in his new process, and soon amateur 'Daguerreotypists' could be seen throughout the city, turning their cameras to the most natural available subject, the views and monuments of Paris. Through their delicate, enchanting photographs a long and powerful association was begun, and the city not only provided an elaborate stage set for the story, but became inextricably linked with it.

The earliest researches were begun by Joseph Nicéphore Niepce as early as 1815 through his work on lithography. The very rudimentary process which Niepce discovered was that when a plate of metal, glass, pewter or even stone, was coated with a light-sensitive varnish and exposed to strong sunlight, the varnish became soluble after being placed in a bath of oil of lavender. The varnish, known as bitumen of Judea, could be found in most etchers' studios as the essential ingredient in preparing copper plates. To Niepce's delight he found it would leave a vague imprint of an image in the areas which had been most exposed once it was washed in the oil of lavender. These *points de vue*, as he was to call them, taken with a camera obscura from the window of his home in Gras, were far from perfect in their reproduction of detail and, even with the modifications he was to bring to them over the next few years, still involved a crude and time-consuming process. There is no doubt, however, that he was the first to witness 'something truly magical' as he described his discovery to his brother. The results of his experiments became known as *héliogravures* and came to the attention of Daguerre in Paris through a famous optician whom both men frequented.

The optician who supplied both Daguerre and Niepce with glasses, lenses and optical instruments was called Charles Chevalier, and his shop was situated on the Quai de l'Horloge. On hearing of the relative similarity of their research on one of his visits to Charles Chevalier, Daguerre decided to write to Niepce suggesting that a joint collaboration might be more fruitful to both of them. Niepce's reception of the proposal was guarded, but he finally agreed to visit the Diorama and was clearly impressed by what he saw. Paris became witness that day in 1827 to a meeting that set in motion a chain of events which, culminating in the announcement of Daguerre's invention more than a decade later, would finally allow us to capture permanently what had fascinated man for so long: the mirror image of our world.

Niepce began collaborating with Daguerre in December 1829. Real advances in their research were made as they experimented with silvered copper plate and iodine crystals, Daguerre bringing funds and enormous energy to their research, as well as the gradually increasing interest of some powerful friends. What they were still unable to achieve, however, and what became the primary area of research, was a method of fixing the image permanently.

When Niepce died suddenly of a stroke in 1833, his son Isidore continued the collaboration with Daguerre and slowly the process was perfected; first by exposing the plates to the vapours of heated mercury, which gave the image finer and greater detail, and then by using a saline solution to fix the image more permanently. Taking their cameras out into the streets of Paris, they tested their discovery, capturing for the first time the likenesses of the Pavillon de Flore, the banks of the Seine and the Pont Neuf. Happy with the result, they baptized it somewhat immodestly the 'daguerreotype'.

Count François Arago, an active politician and a man of scientific learning, came to hear of the invention early in 1839, by which time the Diorama had been destroyed by fire and Daguerre was eager to see his research rewarded. Seeing the enormous potential of the process in the arts and sciences, Arago was able to interest the French state in purchasing it outright. After various demonstrations it was decided that the process would be bought in exchange for life pensions for its two inventors. With Arago's public announcement on 19 August, the invention became official and, wholly unanticipated by its Parisian public, was soon hailed as 'prodigious' and 'a piece of natural magic'. It is easy to understand the enchantment with which the first photographs were received. The images of the city that have been preserved from those early days convey, through their fragility, a Paris of almost ephemeral, ghost-like beauty, enhanced by the absence of human figures which resulted from the long exposure time required to capture movement.

Samuel B. Morse, inventor of the electric telegraph, had the privilege of viewing one of Daguerre's earliest daguerreotypes, 'View from the Boulevard du Temple, Paris 1839', shortly before the invention was publicly launched. In a letter to his brother, he makes mention of the 'astounding precision of the image which contains all the details, even those superfluous to the eye of a painter, and some invisible to the naked eye, but which become perfectly clear when examined under a magnifying glass'. Taken from the window of Daguerre's apartment in the Boulevard St Martin, it has no human figures in it apart from a boot polisher and his client who, whether by accident or design, remained immobile for the duration of the exposure. The daguerreotype was later given to King Louis I of Bavaria by Daguerre as a symbol of the innovative advances in which France was now taking pride.

Despite the excitement that Paris experienced as news of the invention spread, the complexity of the process remained a great disadvantage to the daguerreotype and would detract from its significance in the history of photography. The equipment was cumbersome, and the resulting image, although relatively detailed, was extremely fragile. Its greatest disadvantage, however, was that it was a single, reversed image that could not be duplicated. Moreover, the process was accessible to only a small group of people in the higher echelons of society who could afford the expensive equipment and who had a penchant for chemistry.

The Louvre from the Pavillon de Flore Daguerre 1839

Despite the drawbacks of the daguerreotype, however, Daguerre's commercial acumen helped to proliferate its use, and such was its success that the user's manual which he brought out was reprinted thirty-nine times in two years! The process began to be widely used throughout the world, and daguerreotypes were brought back from as far afield as Columbia (1842) and China (1843).

Daguerre and Niepce, it was soon to be discovered, were not the only people to have come up with a photographic process. During the months preceding Arago's official announcement, Hippolyte Bayard, a clerk in the Ministry of Finance, became fascinated by what he had been hearing in the *salons* of the artist Armaury Duval, which he had been attending. Duval included among his friends an eclectic group of well-known artists and writers to whom the Diorama and Daguerre's experiments would no doubt have been known. Indeed, in early January 1839, six months before its public announcement, Arago had mentioned Daguerre's discovery in passing to the Académie des Sciences, though without divulging any of the details.

It is believed that Bayard, in a very short time, established his own negative process on paper, and soon after, on 20 March 1839, discovered a way in which to print positive images on paper from the negative. He had in fact discovered the basis of the calotype which William Henry Fox Talbot was to perfect in 1841 across the Channel. Bayard, it was later revealed, had even requested an audience with Arago shortly before his official announcement of Daguerre's process, in order to tell him of his discoveries, and at the same time to warn him of the impasse in which Daguerre had placed himself (with the reversed single image on copper plate). Arago, rather than encourage Bayard, dissuaded him from talking about his invention in order not to obstruct the course on which he had embarked with Daguerre. It was unfortunate timing for Bayard, for he gained no recognition for his discovery, but he decided nonetheless to make his own statement by exhibiting, on 24 June 1839, a number of his prints in an auctioneer's saleroom. The latter had been given over to a charity fête in aid of earthquake victims in Martinique. The prints were shown in a single large frame and must have presented a mysterious but beautiful sight to those present. The process did not benefit from the publicity that Daguerre's received, but the exquisite beauty in the detail of his still lives and architectural views was reported in the press. He was to find out to his satisfaction that his work was regarded as having artistic rather than scientific importance, and as such, would open the doors on a whole new context for the medium.

It was not until 1841, when Talbot patented his technique of the calotype (from the Greek *Kalos*, meaning beauty), using paper coated with potassium iodide and silver nitrate thereby rendering it light-sensitive, that Bayard's original process became widely known. It was the first time that it became possible to produce several identical unreversed prints from the same negative image, and it was the advent of this technique that marked the beginning of the era of photography as we know it today. It was only after this that photography really began to proliferate as a medium.

When Talbot decided to visit Paris in 1843 he had perfected his technique and published *The Pencil of Nature*, the first book to contain photographs, pasted in and annotated. He took views from his hotel window and was finally able to see the famous daguerreotypes for himself. Little did he suspect, however, that it was in Paris, away from the restraints that he imposed on the calotype in England (by limiting its use to certain areas of research through the patent he took out), that it would find its most appreciative audience. The success that Hippolyte Bayard was having with his work confirmed that the new art of photography was evolving rapidly.

At the time of the invention of photography, France was ruled by Louis-Philippe. While he instigated few changes in the capital, two of Paris's most notable and much photographed landmarks, though commissioned by earlier kings, were completed under his reign. The Place de la Concorde, so renamed to cleanse the square of the blood spilled during the Revolution, was renovated, and the obelisk, a gift to the Emperor Napoleon from Mehemet Ali, the Viceroy of Egypt, was erected in its centre. The second landmark was the Arc de Triomphe, commissioned by Napoleon at the beginning of the century, and finally unveiled in 1836 after years of neglect.

Louis-Philippe was instrumental, however, in having the first gaslights installed in the city's streets. Invented by Lebon in 1829, but ignored for a decade, gaslight replaced the old and unsatisfactory oil lanterns which were at first positioned on the windowsills and then, around 1769, raised on poles five metres high and sixty metres away from each other. It was said of this system that 'from afar the flame is blinding, close up it gives little light, and beneath it one is in total darkness'.

The stagnating political situation of the time could not have been more conducive to preparing the way for the new art form. Louis-Philippe's conservative monarchy, which came into power in 1830, had few ambitions beyond promoting the security of the upper middle class; a class of respectable merchants and bankers who were themselves anxious not to have their comfortable positions disrupted. In the arts, where a somewhat staid classicism reigned, people were particularly shy of technical innovation. To these people, the advent of photography was of little importance. To those such as Arago, however, who welcomed scientific progress and adhered fervently to the Republican opposition cause, photography represented a powerful new tool.

It did indeed seem tailor-made to their ideals. Grounded in science, it lent itself admirably to the new Realist movement keen to break away from the lofty ideals of high art and the Romantics. Realism, championed by the Barbizon school, turned to nature for its inspiration and sought to imitate it. What better way to achieve this than with the camera? Landscapes, rural scenes and monuments became the obvious subjects for photography; the Realists stressed its social role and its similarities to painting, notably in the use of natural light. Courbet and Millet became excited by the new medium as a means of achieving the desired closeness to nature. Courbet went as far as saying of photography that it was 'by essence the democratic art'. The great precision of the calotype in its faithful reproduction of nature was thus an astounding achievement and soon found a respected place in the arts. A great many painters, aware of the enormous potential which the new medium offered, became photographers and opened studios.

By 1846 Bayard and Talbot's process had become more consistently successful and, as a result, had acquired a number of followers. The process was particularly helped by working modifications published by Louis Blanquart-Evrard, who began to print other photographers' images. Gustave Le Gray's waxed-paper technique (whereby the paper was soaked in melted beeswax before it was coated with collodion) simplified the process even further and allowed photographers to work with ease outdoors, no longer having to carry the heavy developing box, as well as the plates, around with them, for the collodion process did not require the images to be developed immediately. Le Gray was to become one of the great advocates of the artistic merits of photography. He established himself in a studio in the Rue de Richelieu, where he began teaching the art of photography.

Slowly there emerged by the end of the decade a French school of photography that became known throughout the world. Paris had become the natural capital of the new medium which, through the work of photographers such as Baldus, Le Secq, Charles Nègre, Marville, Baron Humbert de Molard and Le Gray, became a new and independent visual language with its own artistic set of rules. Many of the early calotypists had originally been painters and had delighted in their new technique, so appropriate to their naturalistic subjects, and Delaroche, a painter who had a studio in the Institut de France, became eager to initiate his students in the art. Among them were three people who were to become famous for their artistry in the medium; Charles Nègre, Henri Le Secq and an Englishman, Roger Fenton.

Charles Nègre arrived from Cannes in order to pursue his interests in painting and moved into a workshop at 21 Quai de Bourbon on the Ile St Louis, where there already lived a large community of artists and writers including Daumier and

Baudelaire. His interest in photography was without doubt directed towards creating photographic images so that he could use them as working sketches for his paintings. But he soon lost interest in painting and devoted his time entirely to his camera. Nègre would become a familiar figure on the Ile St Louis, at first photographing buildings of architectural interest but soon successfully capturing the very essence of Parisian life itself. One of his most memorable images, that of a horse collapsed on the Quai de Bourbon, caught for the first time all the magic of an actual event and could almost be described as photo-journalistic, had such a style existed.

Henri Le Secq, who would also study under Le Gray, was interested in medieval buildings and cathedrals and was probably aware that many of these buildings were soon to disappear. Le Secq often accompanied Nègre on his many photographic excursions through Paris and occasionally even appears in his photographs. He can be seen in one of Nègre's most stunning images, entitled 'The Vampire', wearing his top hat on the tower of Notre Dame Cathedral. Much of their work was later printed in Blanquart-Evrard's first collection of images: *Paris Photographique* (1851). These early documents of Paris, photographs which reflected the lives of the inhabitants of the city, their appearance and their occupations, testified to a Paris that was to change dramatically over the next few years.

In the face of the official conformism of Louis-Philippe's government, Paris experienced a growth of intellectual and political activity which built up to the February Revolution of 1848. Opposed to the moneyed world of the bourgeois ruling class, young writers and proletarian intellectuals began to meet on the Left Bank, forming a young and Bohemian group known as 'La Jeune France', adamantly asserting their right to create their own aesthetic rules. Many photographers who would later leave their mark belonged to this group. Louis-Philippe soon abdicated in the face of the rebellious uprisings, and Louis-Napoleon was elected later in the year. It was not until 1852, however, that he was officially instated as Napoleon III and Emperor of France.

But photography in Paris had its greatest year still to come. The medium had already been put to such public uses as capturing for posterity the members of the Académie des Sciences, and the collodion technique was about to make photography even more accessible to people from all walks of life. In 1851, its golden year, the Commission des Monuments Historiques formed the Mission Héliographique in order to photograph France's rich architectural heritage; the first institution of its kind to use photography for the purpose of documentation. Five photographers were chosen for the job; Gustave Le Gray, Hippolyte Bayard, Edouard Denis Baldus, Henri Le Secq, and Mestral. The Mission also set out to collect and archive photographs being taken further afield in new and exotic countries. It was around this time that Maxime Du Camp, having learnt the calotype method from Le Gray, travelled to Egypt with his friend Gustave Flaubert.

One of the most important developments of the period was the opening of the first photo printer's workshop by Blanquart-Evrard, also in 1851. He began produc-ing prints in large series, inviting amateur photographers to supply their negatives. It was this group of amateurs that decided in the same year to set up the first photographic society, La Société Héliographique, in the Rue de l'Arcade under the leadership of Baron de Montfort. It became the Société Française de Photographie in 1853, and was a powerful focal point for photographers in Paris. (The society exists under the same name to this day and continues to look after the work taken by the photographers in those early days.) Its members were eminent citizens, such as the optician Charles Chevalier and Eugène Delacroix, and scientists and artists rubbed shoulders with aristocrats. The society's activity was to be 'purely artistic and scientific'; its aim was to help the growth of photography through 'meetings, discussions and exchanges'. The first photographic magazine, *La Lumière*, was also published by the society in the same year.

By the end of 1851 it seemed that a new age had dawned. Men carrying tripods and cameras in the streets of Paris were now a familiar sight. A process known as wet collodion (whereby collodion was used as an invisible substance to hold photosensitive salts to a sheet of glass) began to be used more widely than the calotype, especially by Baldus and Le Gray, the latter having discovered the technique himself in 1849 before Scott Archer in England claimed its invention. The new technique gave their work a moody quality for which they became renowned and which characterized much of the photography of the period.

There was one photographer, however, who contributed more than any other to our collective memory of Old Paris, as the city prior to the Second Empire became known. Charles Marville was another painter and engraver by trade who turned to photography in the late 1840s. His fame rests almost entirely on his photographs of Paris, which capture the melancholy beauty of an irretrievable era. It is the Paris of narrow cobbled streets and crumbling façades; the Paris of Balzac and Victor Hugo. He preferred to work after rain had fallen when the light lent a glistening, irridescent atmosphere of calm to the city. Quite apart from the rich tonal qualities Marville obtained in his prints, he provided an inexhaustible fund of information about the lifestyle of the city's inhabitants, as reflected in the menus posted outside restaurants and on posters advertising the theatrical triumphs of the day.

It would be a mistake, however, to see Marville's photographs as an exercise in facile nostalgia, for he was very much a modernist and a man of his time. He would have participated in the rallies that led Louis-Philippe to abdicate and would have been among those who believed whole-heartedly in the new Realist school of art. His work covered a wide range of subjects in Paris, from demolitions to construction works in progress, parks being landscaped, the new gas street lamps, and the kiosks and *vespasiennes*, or water closets, that were being erected throughout the city. His work was as much a celebration of the new as a mourning of the past.

Most of Marville's Parisian work was instigated by the dramatic changes Napoleon III and his administrator Baron Haussmann brought to the city. Haussmann was made Préfet of the Seine in 1853 by Napoleon and was given the task of transforming the ungovernable medieval city, with its dark and narrow passages awash with waste and its dank culs-de-sacs, into the clean and disease-free city with wide avenues and majestic landmarks that it was to become during the Second Empire.

One of the main urban problems which confronted Napoleon III when he came to power was the enormous growth in population which Paris had experienced in the last few decades, with no corresponding increase in dwellings and amenities. Napoleon's solution, put into action by Haussmann, was to make what were almost surgical incisions into the problem areas with broad boulevards that would open up central Paris and make it accessible to modernization. Water would be brought in, sewers would be laid, street lamps would be installed and public buildings erected. The systematic demolition of much of Old Paris would constitute for Napoleon III a triumph in political reasoning, since the ideals were humanitarian and not only would the out-of-work be employed in the rebuilding of their city, but he would also have gained effective political control over its inhabitants. Above all, he would be left with 'the most splendid and most salubrious of the capitals of Europe' (Napoleon III, 1866).

When work began, it seemed that Paris had inadvertently taken a step backwards. Living space became even more at a premium as people squatted in courtyards and the city took on the aspect of a never-ending building site. On the Ile de la Cité, the demolition was quite ruthless. Haussmann removed about ninety streets – homes, shops, taverns and all – and twenty-five thousand people, in the cause of opening up the views of Notre Dame. Fortunately he did understand the fact that a respect for the past made for a greater

Public urinal
Marville 1870

future. It was for this reason that from his offices at the Hôtel de Ville he engaged archivists to document the aspects of the city that were to be destroyed. Among those he chose was Charles Marville, who had already made a name for himself with his architectural views, notably of cathedrals in Germany. Having worked with paper negatives, which he gave to Blanquart-Evrard to print, he switched to the new collodion method and began his documentation of Paris in 1856. In the same year he was to be one of three photographers to cover the baptism of the Prince Imperial. It would seem from his extensive archives that he had initially begun documenting the changes taking place purely for his own purposes, and that the Préfecture, on hearing of his work, commissioned him to continue with his documentation. He became known as the 'Photographer of the City of Paris', not simply for administrative reasons but because his *oeuvre* was to stretch over nearly twenty years.

The Paris World Fair of 1855 was an important landmark in the history of photography, marking its transition from an art form practised by an elite group of scientifically minded people to a commercial and industrial practice which took it into a new age. It was the first time that photographs were publicly exhibited and had a special section allocated to them. It included work by the Bisson brothers and even Millet, for whom photography had an enormous appeal. By now the Realist movement had many followers, and the public came in large numbers to admire the new artistic creations that photography allowed. Another reason for the great interest in the work shown at the fair was its inclusion of a number of portraits. Present at the opening was a figure who went by the title of 'The Emperor's Photographer' and who, it appeared, had been made the fair's official photographer. His name was André-Adolphe Disderi. On his arrival in Paris in the previous year, he had patented a system which allowed him to print a series of portraits of a relatively small format on the same collodion negative. These were then glued on to a light cardboard backing and sold as calling cards at a very low cost. Disderi had unwittingly brought to Paris an element which was to revolutionize the use of photography and win the respect and appreciation of the masses through its appeal to man's social and narcissistic nature. Napoleon III became a much-photographed Emperor, the sale of family photograph albums boomed, and people queued at the famous studios to have their 'trivial image' (Baudelaire) captured for posterity.

With the portrait photograph all the rage, the number of studios grew dramatically. From twenty-nine in 1851 there were as many as one hundred and sixty by 1856, and the number increased fivefold again over the next ten years. In 1860 photography offered relatively good profits in return for a relatively low capital investment, and it attracted people from occupations as diverse as engineering, teaching and dentistry. A visit to one of these portrait photographers became almost obligatory for the Parisian bourgeoisie intent on keeping up social pretensions, especially as the settings for the portraits were usually more luxurious than the sitters' own homes. Studios such as that of Disderi, situated on two floors on the Boulevard des Italiens, were often luxurious affairs, employed many people (Disderi at one time employed over a hundred people, producing up to two thousand images a day) and were elaborately decorated with the necessary accessories for use as backdrops. The photographic sessions would take place at the time when Parisians would be promenading along the boulevards or at the time of the evening theatre shows, so as to enhance the social importance of the occasion.

Félix Nadar was a man of many talents who became a great portraitist. He set up his studio at 35 Boulevard des Capucines in a building of steel and glass which was an even more extravagant affair than Disderi's, with Gobelins tapestries, a bubbling fountain, Chinese staircase and artefacts. Hanging on the façade of the building was a sign which depicted his name in large red letters illuminated by gaslight. Gaspard Félix Tournachon, known as Nadar, had originally been a journalist and part of the Bohemian intellectual set. An enormously successful socialite, he attracted the *beau monde* of Parisian society and his individual portraits were expensive. He was on intimate terms with Offenbach, Baudelaire, Delacroix, Dumas and de Vigny, and his photographic sessions were the talk of Paris. This was to be of enormous value to him as, with the proliferation of images of the Emperor and the Empress being sold, it became a matter of pride for the famous to have their likeness on sale. Not unnaturally, the photographer's renown increased according to the fame of the people he photographed.

The IX*e arrondissement* became the fashionable area for the studios or *ateliers*, as they were known, and drew many who came with high hopes of making their fortune. Etienne Carjat, a close friend of Verlaine's, set up in the Rue Lafitte; Pierre Petit in the Place Cadet, Crépieu in the Rue Frochot and Adam Salomon on the Rue de la Rochefoucauld. The firm of Mayer & Pierson, established in 1855, was a highly respected commercial enterprise which became the official photographer to the Royal Houses of Portugal, Norway and Sweden. Present at the baptism of the Prince Imperial, they were to catalogue the Prince's childhood at regular intervals until their closure in 1865. There even appeared a number of travelling portrait photographers who covered fairs and country fêtes, offering almost instantaneous photographs which, in the more rural areas where people were less well informed of the recent technical wonders of the city, would readily be accepted as icons. Photography had truly entered a 'popular age'.

Nadar was an engaging and enterprising character. He distinguished himself from his contemporaries by his interest in the psychological element of portraiture and showed great sensitivity towards his subjects. His photographs exuded simplicity and sincerity. Not only was he the first photographer to go down the catacombs to photograph by spotlight; he was probably also the first to produce an aerial view from a hot air balloon above Paris when, in 1856, he took views of the Arc de Triomphe and the Bois de Boulogne.

By the 1860s, Napoleon III's liberal regime was in full bloom. The Second Empire gave privileges to the middle classes who, quick to capitalize on their new-found favour, sometimes amassed colossal fortunes. One of the negative effects of Haussmann's rebuilding of Paris, however, despite the benefits of gaslight in the streets and sanitary canalization, was the systematic and sometimes needless destruction of buildings and monuments of great architectural interest. Ten churches on the Ile St Louis alone were destroyed, and many of the *hôtels particuliers*, the noble town dwellings of the Marais, were also torn down. While the *nouveaux riches* indulged in their new privileges, with parties and travel to foreign countries, the immediate effects of the urbanization were detrimental to the poor. Many of them lost jobs as machines took over, social benefits did not as yet exist, and more often than not they were relocated in conditions even more appalling in the city's east end than they had known in the heart of Old Paris.

During the late 1850s another trend swept through Paris; the sterioscopic photograph. Invented by Charles Brewster in England in 1852, the camera used a reduced focal system and was thus the first photographic device to capture the movement of people with any precision. The public displayed a fascination with seeing the banks of the Seine and the boulevards of Paris, now filled with people. Two photographers by the name of Soulier and Ferrier were to use sterioscopy to great aesthetic advantage and in 1860 produced a series of images of which it was reported in the press that one could see 'thousands of walking people and moving vehicles and not one blurred. Even figures standing in the shade can be observed in detail, and this with an exposure time that does not exceed a fraction of a second.'

In 1862 Hippolyte Jouvin produced a collection of over two hundred views, which he called *Vues Instantanées de Paris*, and which met with enormous popular success. The views included parades and fairs and captured for the first time Paris as it really was, a city thronging with people and slowly beginning to play a leading role in matters of fashion and style. The popularity of the sterioscopic system was greatly enhanced by an invention which took place in Belleville, in the north-east of Paris, shortly afterwards. A system put together by Jules Richard allowed the photograph to be viewed through an optical device which restored depth of field and relief to an image, thereby creating a three-dimensional effect; he called it the Verascope.

While the portraitist quickly won the hearts of the Parisians, photographers such as Le Gray and Le Secq, although they continued to work, were very much out of the limelight. Le Gray, disgruntled over the commercialization of photography, moved his studio from the Rue de Richelieu to the Boulevard des Capucines near the church of La Madeleine. The Bisson brothers were soon to follow, occupying studios in the same building and taking to exhibiting large prints of their work. A fourth photogra-

pher, by the name of De Marnhy, known for his work on photo-sculpture, was also to move in. As a result of the intense concentration of photographic talent, Le Gray's studio attracted an important following among those dissatisfied with the more commercial course photography had been taking.

With the Second Empire, the intellectual elite had slowly been losing favour as the more conservative bourgeois public voiced their opinions. Victor Hugo went into exile in Guernsey; Baudelaire's *Les Fleurs du Mal* was considered morally offensive, and Flaubert's *Madame Bovary* came under heavy moral criticism, finally forcing him into the courtroom to defend its publication. The group of studios thus took on the atmosphere of a *salon* of dissident artists and drew such writers as Théophile Gautier, Honoré de Balzac and Janin, the critic, who all came to view and discuss the latest

Batignolles
Bayard 1839

work. The more illustrious were invited to choose among those exhibited and were presented with free prints. It could not have been more of an antithesis to Disderi's commercial studio, but it sadly reflected their poor business sense, a factor now vital to survival. These photographers who championed an aesthetic vision for photography were the last to do so in a trade which was rapidly becoming impersonal. Indeed, Nadar later confided to his son Paul that, after the exhilarating first few years, the business of portrait photography could only start, at best, with an attitude of inspired indifference, before it turned to aversion and finally horror. Of the photographers who had been chosen to document the French architectural patrimony for the Mission Héliographique, Charles Nègre was to do little of consequence after 1860; Le Secq stopped taking photographs after 1856; and Baldus took none after the mid-1860s. Le Gray, following the financial failure of his studio on the Boulevard des Capucines, left his family to go to Egypt, where he became a drawing teacher. He died in 1882 after a fall from his horse. Only Hippolyte Bayard continued for over thirty years to take new and exciting photographs.

Anyone predicting, in the summer of 1870, that Paris would be under siege in a matter of a few weeks, would have been ridiculed. For Paris had become, thanks to the changes instigated by Napoleon III, the *Ville Lumière*, the cosmopolitan capital of the world and the queen of civilized cities.

But matters deteriorated rapidly. Although Paris had been a fortified city since 1840, its fortifications had been badly neglected and it very quickly became apparent that the city would have to prepare for a siege as the Prussians approached. Over three thousand heavy guns were brought into Paris; the Louvre was turned into an armaments factory, the Gare d'Orléans into a balloon factory, and the Gare de Lyon into a cannon foundry. The Bois de Boulogne was given over to grazing for sheep and oxen, and flourmills were set up in the Gare du Nord. The Emperor offered to surrender on 2 September and the Second Empire was inevitably overthrown two days later. The Third Republic was immediately proclaimed and on the same day Victor Hugo, France's greatest Republican and the Empire's most famous exile, returned to a tumultuous welcome. The French troops that had not been engaged in battle returned hastily to man the defences, but by 19 September the city was under siege.

Nadar was one of the few photographers to capitalize on the situation, as most others had fled the city. As commander of the newly formed Balloon Corps, he arranged for the first postal balloon to leave Paris from Montmartre five days after the siege began. With his customary showmanship, he dropped four thousand of his visiting cards over the Prussian lines, each with one corner turned down in the ritual manner.

The last of the barricades
Bayard 1848

The siege of Paris lasted longer than anyone ever imagined it would. As winter drew on the Prussians began to shell the city and most of the French military operations were proving futile; by 27 January the government had capitulated and through the ensuing peace negotiations lost Alsace and Lorraine. To the outrage of the people, Thiers agreed to a triumphal entry by the enemy troops into the city. As it turned out, however, Paris had withstood the German siege better than it did the class differences that were made evident during the struggle. The result was inevitable, and on 18 March revolution flared up in the city. The government fled to Versailles and the Commune of Paris was proclaimed.

Few photographers had remained during the siege and subsequent revolution. Disderi photographed the barricades and the Home Guard on sentry duty. Pierre Petit photographed Thiers's house after it was destroyed by the Commune. A man called Liébert, about whom little is known, succeeded in photographing the Communards outside the Hôtel de Ville and in the Place de la Concorde, and a marvellous series of images was taken by Bracquehais of the Colonne Vendôme being pulled down.

Courbet, as one of the main instigators, is seen standing beside the column. Bracquehais appears to have been the only photographer of renown not to have fled the capital during the insurrection, and he tirelessly covered the city from one end to the other, photographing the cannons of the Communards, barricades and bomb sites. They appear to have been taken purely for personal interest and he seems to have found it satisfying to be harnessing the innovation of photography, with the camera's power as a witness, to convey the horror of the period. Following Charles Nègre, Bracquehais was another precursor of photo-journalism.

When the city's inhabitants returned, photography took on a very different role. The Commune had lasted some seventy days before it was quashed but had managed to wreak an inordinate amount of devastation on the city; there was, as a result, a rush of activity as photographers hurried to capture on their glass plates the gutted Hôtel de Ville, razed to the ground by the Communards, and the smoking mounds of rubble of the Palais des Tuileries, until recently the Emperor's palace. Photography was being used, for the first time, as an instrument of propaganda. Some went even further, such as Appert with his photo-montages, by literally distorting images in order to exaggerate the Communards' crimes. A small industry of photographic material, in the form of books and postcards of the scenes of destruction, appeared on the market shortly afterwards. Disderi published *Ruines de Paris et ses Environs*, and Pierre Petit published *Recueil de Paris Brûlé*.

Photography was to reach a new market towards the late 1870s, and grow away once more from the artistic institutions towards the commercial. It had become possible to produce reproduction prints at low cost and still retain the quality of the original print. Magazines began to bring out sepia-toned prints which were hand-pasted on to the pages. One of them, *Galerie Contemporaine*, chose to produce a series on specific subjects, and often featured work by Nadar, Carjat and Pierre Petit, as well as many other well-known portraitists of the day.

Louis-Alphonse Poitevin, a chemist working from his studio in the Rue du Faubourg St Jacques, soon after brought out the photo-typogravure, finally making it possible to reproduce photographs in the newspapers. It was on 5 September 1886 that Paul Nadar, son of Félix Nadar, arranged an interview between his father and Eugène Chevreul, a highly respected scientist of ninety-three. Chevreul was photographed as he spoke, with all the spontaneity of expression and gesture, and a series of twelve pages was published by the photogravure technique in the *Journal Illustré*. Within a few months, a number of magazines and newspapers, such as *Paris Moderne*, began to use photographs as an alternative to illustration.

The period that followed was uneventful for photography. The portrait photographers returned to their studios and continued to find favour with the Parisians. The artistic circles had almost disappeared; Nadar moved to more modest premises in the Rue d'Anjou; Disderi was unable to withstand the strong competition and died destitute. The golden age of portraiture had stifled its own progenitors, and photography as an art was stagnating. It would require the imagination of George Eastman, with the invention of the Kodak camera and all the technical advances that it entailed, to shake photography out of its mediocrity.

Place de la Bastille
Melby (attrib.) 1848

Street Scene
Fox Talbot 1843

Funeral awnings in the Rue des Batignolles
Bayard 1845

The fall of a horse
Nègre *c*.1851

The Vampire
Nègre *c.*1853

Passing through the gate
Bertsch 1855

Pont Neuf
Seeberger 1910

Institut de France, Pont du Louvre
Marville 1853

Marville's studio on the Boulevard Saint-Jacques
Marville *c.*1867

Public baths
Le Secq 1852

From top left, clockwise: Passage du Dragon c.1860; Impasse des Bourdonnais c.1858;
Hôtel Dieu, view from the Quai de Montebello c.1858; Rue Chanoinesse c.1858
Marville

Tuileries
Anon. 1867

Palais du Louvre
Baldus 1852–7

Pont Neuf and Quai du Louvre
Anon. 1845–50

Avenue du Bois de Boulogne
Lartigue 1911

ATGET & THE TURN OF THE CENTURY
1889 ► 1918

Place Saint-Medard
Atget 1899

W/hen Richard Leach Maddox invented the dry gelatin plate in 1871, he can hardly have been aware that he was laying the foundation for a revolution in the way photography would be used. Nor did he know that he would take photography out of the doldrums, and nowhere more so than in Paris, where it seemed that only portrait photographers existed. The years since its invention had seen the medium grow through a difficult adolescence; the turn of the century would see it through to maturity.

While Maddox was promoting the dry plate in England, George Eastman, an amateur photographer in the USA who was finding the wet plate messy and inconvenient, heard of the advances that were being made, tried them himself and was soon selling his dry plates to his friends around Rochester. The advent of the dry plate made life much easier for the photographer, who no longer needed to be within easy reach of a darkroom. Now, instead of being a ten-minute time-bomb, a photograph could be developed and printed at a later stage. The widespread use of the dry plate by the mid-1880s provides the clearest evidence of the new simplicity it had brought to the medium.

The development of emulsion film, which was sensitive to speed and movement, was fundamental to many of the developments in photography which took place in the late nineteenth century, but particularly in the analysis of motion. When the photographic emulsions became sensitive enough to record movement with a certain precision, it became clear that there were discrepancies between what the naked eye perceived and what the camera saw. Eadweard Muybridge's experiments with the trotting horse, Occident, are famous for what they revealed: that the 'rocking-horse' position of the horses in the paintings by Edgar Degas, and other painters before him, was in fact wrong. When he visited Paris he was greeted, even by the renowned horse painters, as a hero. Muybridge's work with Occident, which was to develop into an eleven-volume compendium called *Animal Locomotion*, had in fact been instigated by Lelan Stanford, Governor of California and President of the Central Pacific Railroad. Stanford had heard of the work of a young Parisian physiologist, Etienne-Jules Marey, on animal motion – specifically on the trotting position of the horse – and commissioned Muybridge to make his own investigations. Marey no doubt met Muybridge during his visit to Paris, as he was inspired to devise his own photographic systems in order to study the flight pattern of birds. Over the next few years Marey perfected the 'photographic gun' and the 'chronophotograph', with which he was able to obtain, with a single camera, by a process of superimposition on one dry plate, a 'multiple' image. His photographs of a running man or of a trotting horse thus convey the various stages of motion in a single image. The ground he covered in his research was to lead indirectly to the invention of the motion picture by the Lumière brothers a few years later in 1895.

Another effect of the dry plate, in its scientific role, was to bring a new thoroughness to a medium which would henceforth become an investigative tool. A whole new range of subjects that lent themselves to spontaneity and improvisation were now presented to the photographer. However, while the dry-plate process had indeed simplified matters greatly, for the time being its use still required a certain technical competence and interest on the part of the photographer. In the meantime, George Eastman had been experimenting with a system which would simplify matters further: the flexible negative. What he came up with, however, was a somewhat delicate procedure which involved soaking a gelatin emulsion from its paper support, and mounting it on glass plate. Feeling that he could not guarantee that his clients would get it right, he decided to do the processing himself in his factory. In 1888, in conjunction with the new negative, he launched the camera which changed everything. The Kodak was the first 'hand-held' camera on the market, and he was to say of it that anyone who could wind a watch could use it. The 'little black box' was sometimes no bigger than 3 × 6 inches, but the 'snapshot' produced a detailed image, arresting any subject so as to give it no visible trace of movement. It came with one hundred exposures of film which could be returned for processing to Eastman's factory, together with the camera, which would be reloaded with a new film and sent back while the first was being processed. Eastman's slogan 'You press the button; we do the rest' had brought photography into the modern age.

In Paris, Paul Nadar, who had taken over his father's studio in 1876, became Eastman's exclusive selling agent in France. His aim was to promote the 'journalism of tomorrow' with the help of the new Eastman products. The Kodak camera could take pictures in normal light with a shutter speed as fast as 1/500th of a second, so that a tripod was no longer necessary. Photography had been brought to the masses and, more importantly, into the home. It left the lofty realms of wealthy professional circles to enter the world of the amateur, for the new owners of the Kodak camera were primarily people interested in taking souvenir photographs of the family and friends and the famous monuments they visited on their holidays. Soon the family album was all the rage, with snapshots of the baby's christening, the wedding or the birthday party.

At the same time that the Kodak camera was being promoted with great fervour by Paul Nadar, the Parisian skyline was about to be dramatically altered by the construction of the Eiffel Tower. There was a time when the Champ de Mars, the site that was chosen for its construction, was made up of rolling fields. The area had been cleared in the eighteenth century for military manoeuvres and had also served as a practice ground for the first ballooning attempts. It was only during the Second Empire that the open parkland opposite the Ecole Militaire was landscaped and began to be used for horse racing. It later became the scene of the World Fairs, and it was in anticipation of the 1889 Fair that it was decided that a spectacular edifice should be built to commemorate the event.

Construction of the Eiffel Tower began in 1887 amid much protest. A petition was immediately signed by a hundred respected figures from different academic fields in an attempt to stop the work. Verlaine called it 'a skeleton of a belfry'. Huysmans called it 'a hideous edifice of wire and steel tubing resembling a factory building'. The project was eventually passed, however, and it took seven thousand tons of steel, two and a half million rivets, and three hundred construction workers working for eighteen months, to complete. At its opening in 1889 it stood almost a thousand feet high and was the tallest building in the world.

One can also safely say that most visitors would have been eager to photograph it for their family album. As a result, the Eiffel Tower can be assumed to have used up more of George Eastman's film than almost any other monument in the world.

Emile Zola, fascinated by the new medium, was one of the earliest to take up photography as a hobby and became a great chronicler of Paris at the turn of the century. He could easily have been mistaken for a professional: by 1888 he possessed eight cameras and two darkrooms, and over the next seven years he was to produce as many as seven thousand glass plates. In his style and approach to photography, however, he was a true amateur, for he would go everywhere with his cameras taking snapshots of his family, daily events in the city and his favourite promenading haunts of the Tuileries and the banks of the Seine. (The term 'snapshot' was probably taken from its use in hunting, where it refers to the hasty firing of a shot at a moving target without taking deliberate aim.) Zola, despite his enthusiasm, was not concerned with the artistry or the polemics of photography; he excelled in the type of amateur photographs taken on a Sunday afternoon walk with the family. If he had an interest in the development of photography it was through his friends at the Café Guerbois, near the Place de Clichy, where he had been introduced to Nadar and Carjat. The café was a favourite meeting-place for 'Les Refusés', a group of contemporary artists whose name was derived from their rejection by the artistic circles of the time. They included Monet, Renoir, Degas, Manet and Sisley, and the future achievements of Les Refusés became history. But in 1874 they had been refused an exhibition by the Louvre and turned to their friend Nadar, who lent them his studio in the Boulevard des Capucines as a venue.

Fin-de-siècle Paris was not merely the end of a century in a particular city. The turn of the century marked the middle of a remarkable epoch in a more than remarkable city. It began with the death of Victor Hugo in 1885 and was to draw to a close with the First World War. The Second Empire, together with the Franco-Prussian war, had left Parisians with a deep sense of defeat and insecurity. To many it seemed a city without hope. In fact, out of this sense of loss Paris grew with renewed vigour and success. Far from being the lifeless capital so many predicted it would be, it was to live a period of its history known as 'La Belle Epoque' for which it would always be remembered. It would thrive on all levels; in philosophy, science, medicine and technology. The literary scene also contained a wealth of talent: Mallarmé, Verlaine, Rimbaud, Anatole France, Gide, Cocteau and Proust all contributed to the period's aesthetic richness and were subject to its influence.

In art the sense of renewal was even more pronounced. The breakaway from the academic *salons* of Ingres and Delacroix was definitive, and Impressionism became well and truly established. Numerous artists found fame for themselves at this time, including Cézanne, Degas, Gauguin, Renoir, Rousseau and Matisse. Paris was their inspiration, and the fervour of the time drew many others. Bakst and Chagall came from Russia; De Chirico and Modigliani from Italy; Juan Gris and Picasso from Spain.

Living in Paris as the new century began was a young boy of seven whose passion it was to take photographs. His name was Jacques-Henri Lartigue, and he was probably the most representative of the early amateurs who could not resist keeping a photographic diary of their daily activities. Born in 1894 into a wealthy upper-middle-class family, he was given his first camera by his father, who was himself fascinated by photography and took it upon himself to develop his son's snapshots. Lartigue's *milieu* was the charming world of the privileged during the last years of the Belle Epoque, of motor car rides and afternoons promenading in the Bois de Boulogne with his nanny.

The early photographs of Lartigue testify to the shift the medium had made towards the informal, both in the way photographs were taken and in their subject-matter. Not only is the angle of the photograph dependent on the size of a boy of seven, it is also dependent on the subject a boy would choose to photograph. There are the inevitable photographs of his toys taken while lying on the floor, or of himself in the bath at water level. Lartigue handled the camera with a charming insouciance for composition or form, and he used it spontaneously to photograph exactly what he pleased. The photographs he was to take were in a sense a child's recognition of moments that delighted him, and which he wished to record in his 'memory box'.

The Avenue du Bois was one of the favourite promenading avenues in Paris at the turn of the century. Frequented by pedestrians, horsemen, carriages and motor cars, it presented for the young Lartigue a splendid source of material. As one of his companions explained many years later, 'The elegant lady strollers would descend the Avenue du Bois, walk or drive down to the gates of the Avenue des Acacias and return as many times as they could, in order to look, to greet passers-by, to be looked at, to pass again and greet once more. Some stayed in their cars or carriages, others, especially if they had a pretty dress to show off, would alight.'

Races at Auteuil
Lartigue 1911

Lartigue was to spend many afternoons fascinated by the elegance and coquetterie of these ladies, photographing them wearing the latest fashion. He would sit in ambush, awaiting 'the pheasant in the chicken run', delighting as much in photographing a ridiculous hat perched on the head of some eccentric woman as in finding himself face to face with a lady of exquisite beauty and elegance. The freshness of these documents emanates from the unselfconscious nature of his treatment of his subjects. In his notebooks one may read: 'Idea: photograph Bichonnade and mother when they are wearing their hats'; or 'Another idea: Why not photograph the most eccentric hats in the Bois de Boulogne?'. It is easy to see how a boy of his age would find ladies and their hats amusing subjects; especially as the Belle Epoque favoured extravagant creations with ostrich feathers, veils and fox tails. His other favourite subjects were his cat Zizi, his nanny Dudu, and all the familiar components of his private world, which he photographed with an extraordinary precision. He would leave nothing to chance and calculated the distance and shutter speed with great care, always capturing movement at its most emphatic and from the most humorous of angles.

The combination of diaries, drawings and photographs (250,000 in all) was to become a charmingly intimate record of society life at the turn of the century. It remained an entirely personal enterprise, and he continued to organize his photographs into their respective archives many years later. Lartigue became a painter and illustrator by profession, however, and photography always remained an enjoyable hobby for him; an amateur, secondary exercise which was only brought to the public's attention after the Second World War by Richard Avedon. It was he who introduced Lartigue to the work of Proust, whom he had never heard of despite the close similarity of their worlds.

The photographic market was soon to be flooded with all kinds of different portable equipment, and manufacturers such as Belliéni and Carpentier brought out more and more ingenious portables. Every new model had some new feature to commend it. By the 1890s reflex cameras of the Graflex type were popular for their ability to project the image right side up on to the plate until the shutter was released. The parks and streets of Paris were now full of the new breed of amateur photographers, arranging their families in front of various monuments in order to have their portraits taken.

With the passage of time, it became apparent that Paris had more to be proud of than it had previously thought. The changes instigated by Napoleon III were coming into their own. The boulevards no longer seemed like brash incisions into the heart of the old city and became the life and soul of Parisian social life. The promenade became as socially important as having one's portrait taken had been a few years before. The city was also undergoing changes as a result of the arrival of the motor car; by 1900 the horse-drawn bus had given way to the Métropolitain, and the electric street lamp had taken the place of gas.

But it was not so much in its external aspects as in the rhythm of life that the city was changing, and no one documented that change with more sensitivity than a photographer whom the Belle Epoque chose more or less to ignore. For this reason we know relatively little about Eugène Atget, except that he arrived in Paris in 1896 from Bordeaux at the age of forty, with a mistress some twelve years older than he, and a few savings. Whether it was his deep disillusionment with his career in the theatre that brought him to Paris or, like so many others, the hope that with the artistic fervour which was gripping the capital he might also find success as a painter, we shall never know. But, if so, he was to be disappointed, for he found that he could neither make a living from, nor express his artistic vision through painting. He did, however, frequent the Bohemian *ateliers* in Montmartre and became acquainted with some of its painters, which was to stand him in good stead when he decided to take up photography in 1898. He gave himself the rather ambiguous title of 'Photographe d'Art', taking a studio at 31 Rue Campagne Première, which was later to become famous for the number of photographers who lived there, and posted a sign on the door which read: 'Documents pour Artistes'.

Atget's work was motivated by two factors; the commercial and the socio-aesthetic. While frequenting artists' studios in Montmartre, he had discovered that many of them required photographs of a wide variety of subjects to use as reference material for their painting. Braque and Utrillo began to buy prints of street scenes in Montmartre from him, which provided a small income and allowed him to pursue his new *métier*, for Atget had clearly been searching for a way to convey his own vision of the world. We learn from his writings that from the very beginning he had the intention of collating everything which he considered 'artistic or picturesque in and around Paris'. Over the next twenty years he was to produce one of the most formidable catalogues of photographic history covering the transition of the city from the nineteenth into the twentieth century.

Atget's documenting of Paris was painstakingly extensive. It included views as well as façades, and in particular the small trades that had all but died out, and their way of life. Whereas Marville had photographed Paris thirty years earlier using wet plates, Atget used dry plates. With the advantages the new method presented, he was able to treat the same subjects repeatedly from different angles and in different lights. It is apparent from his work that he came to realize that the most interesting distinctions in photography were not categorical but dependent on the photographer's attention to his subject. He was known to photograph the same views at different times of day in the knowledge that a photographic subject was never the same on two occasions. Through this realization he became, unwittingly, a modern artist.

Baker
Atget 1898

He was to become a familiar figure around Montparnasse, hunched over his tripod with his black cloak over his shoulders. He would also have seemed an eccentric photographer for his day, since many of them had by this time taken to the infinitely more manageable hand-held camera. He usually rose before dawn so as to avoid the shadows cast by the traffic on the scenes he wished to capture, carrying his large and antiquated 18 × 24 centimetre glass plates in a box over his shoulder. But despite his old-fashioned equipment, he was still able to capture his subjects with great freshness and precision.

Atget effectively harnessed the enormously evocative power of the photographic image. Each one of his photographs goes beyond being a simple document. Nothing is superfluous to the whole, and through his unflagging passion for his work we are witness to the lives of butchers, cobblers and merchants of Paris, of florists and errand boys. His photographs were never isolated instances, but always went to make up a greater whole, alternating between close-up and distanced views. Anxious to convey the city in its developing or deteriorating stages, Atget also photographed monuments and buildings in their various stages of construction or demolition. There is rarely a reference to the present in his photographs, and contemporary connotations are usually avoided, which lends his work a certain timelessness. He never, for instance, photographed the Eiffel Tower, perhaps preferring to show the essential, intimate side of Paris which formed its living structure, rather than what was immediately obvious.

A notable characteristic of the age was the desire to create order through a catalogued system of documentation. This became Atget's overriding passion, his aim being to provide an overview of the city of Paris, a collective whole which confirmed the universality of a subject rather than its individuality.

The first decade of the twentieth century was not an easy time for a photographer to make a living. With the exception of portrait studios, the market for photography as an artistic profession was practically non-existent. Slowly, but consistently, Atget began to sell his photographs – mostly of buildings of architectural importance, churches, fountains and other monuments – to museums and other institutions. As someone who had barely been able to make a living for the first half of his life, Atget was particularly proud to have found a livelihood he was passionate about and which also paid the rent. His work was to straddle two very different epochs, and indeed his story will be picked up again in the Paris of the Surrealists. The First World War was to see him destitute again, but Atget persevered with his documentation regardless of events taking place around him, whether in photography or in the world at large. Over the years the influence of Atget has reached almost mythical proportions, with every new group attempting to enlist his work in defence of their own intentions or to project on to him artistic intentions which he didn't have. He remained a documentalist pure and simple in his vision and never diverted from his primary objective, which was to capture the evolution of the city in which he lived.

By contrast, Lartigue's progress as a photographer during the years leading up to the war, while the amateur market flourished, was simply a function of his growing up. His interest in kites developed into an interest in the early flying machines; his interest in box carts grew into a passion for motor cars. His vision remained a witty one, and his use of the camera was an inextricable element of his life. What experimentation there was in his photographs related to movement, but such experiments arose more from a desire to record the situation at hand than from an analytical interest in the medium.

Louis Vert, a student of Pierre Petit and essentially a printer, had much more of an analytical interest in capturing human movement. The early years of the twentieth century saw the appearance in Paris of the Guido-Sigriste, an instrument of extraordinary precision for its day, which permitted an exposure time of 1/5000th of a second. This enabled Louis Vert to become one of the best documentors of the inhabitants of the city. Unlike Marville's photographs which are often devoid of human presence, Vert's work conveys turn-of-the-century Paris with all the style and excitement for which it was becoming known. His photographs include military parades in all their detailed splendour and scenes from his daily excursions along the banks of the Seine. Being a great amateur of horse racing, he, like Lartigue, would spend the afternoons in the Bois de Boulogne at the races. In contrast to Lartigue, however, whose main source of inspiration was the fashion and elegance of the spectators, Louis Vert was more intent on capturing the moving crowds and the races themselves.

Towards the end of the nineteenth century, partly owing perhaps to a collective nostalgia in the face of a changing world and the social transformations created by industrialization, a sociological desire had arisen to classify people as well as things. Photography was a natural vehicle for this, and was used in many different contexts, soon becoming popular, for example, with travellers to foreign and unexplored countries. One of its more unlikely uses had been by a Parisian Police Inspector. Alphonse Bertillon, who was interested in the technical advances of photography and its uses, had set up a statistically based filing system using photography. Any individual suspected of a criminal act was photographed from several different angles, and the documents were kept on file.

When photography wasn't being put to practical uses, the photographs which began to appear on the market testified to the new role the photographer himself was to play. He became the protagonist, abandoning the black cape, able to approach his subject freely and participate in the image by defining his own position. There was a fundamental shift in people's assumption of the basic principles of the medium. The camera with the new emulsion film was now able to capture what the naked eye could not see, and it could be captured by anyone, anywhere. There was no need for prior knowledge of the medium, nor for a studio, and to its artistic heritage was added a new-found freedom of observation. There was also a fundamental change in subject-matter. With the exception of Atget's work, which was only brought to the public's attention a decade later, photographs ceased to be the elaborate, posed records of visual data. Landscapes and formal architectural views lost the power to fascinate; photographing had become a personally and emotionally based act of recording the more inconsequential elements of life.

Despite the enormous commercialization which the hand-held camera brought about and the attempts to standardize the key elements, there was, as might be expected, a movement against the intrusion of the amateur into the world of the professional and an attempt to regain the medium's former mystery and magic. The change in direction raised once again the question which had been all important since the beginnings of photography: whether or not it might be considered an art on the level of painting.

Ironically, many of the new movement's supporters were artists who had come to the medium through the very fact that it had been made accessible by the advent of the hand-held camera. Vuillard was to use the camera in much the same way as Lartigue had done, but with the purpose of observing the possible subjects of his painting in different ways and from different points of view. His motivation was primarily artistic, but his use of the camera confirmed the new way in which photographs were being taken. Degas had also taken to using the camera to help him with compositions, and Bonnard, between 1898 and 1908, made constant use of his Kodak. In particular, he took a series of nudes in his apartment in Paris, between 1899 and 1901, which marked the beginnings of the fundamental change his painting was to undergo during this period. As Bonnard later wrote, most artists would use photography 'to remember what had caught their attention and make a note of it as quickly as possible'.

A strange and perhaps unexpected attribute of the hand-held camera was its power of intrusion. It had become so small and manageable that photographers were able to use the camera almost unnoticed, and sometimes in situations which were not appropriate. This aspect of photography would come to be thought of as a characteristic of the press, and would create its own particular photographic style. When Paul Nadar had spoken of the 'journalism of tomorrow', he was referring chiefly to a new breed of 'reporters' that had steadily been growing since the half-tone process, which allowed limitless cheap reproductions, had opened up the possibility of printing photographs in the press. They lay in wait for events of journalistic importance, and acquired a taste for the sensational. One such event took place in October 1895, when a train failed to stop at the Gare Montparnasse and plunged down into the street; this was the kind of subject that found its way on to the covers of the new magazines which enjoyed such popularity during the Belle Epoque. Greatly assisted by the technical advances in photography, the 'reporters' found themselves at the beginning of a long and powerful tradition which was to play a major role in photography in Paris.

It is perhaps in the notion of the greater personal vision, as already noted in the work of Atget, that we may find the roots of the movement which was to dominate the scene in photography for the next decade and regain for professional photography some of the limelight which had been stolen by amateurs. Whereas with Atget the desire to go beyond mere representation of the facts, by incorporating a personal vision, may not have been conscious, with Peter Henry Emerson the process was rendered whole-heartedly conscious by stressing the subjective element in photography and differentiating between the camera vision, devoid of human sentiment, and the human vision.

The movement which became known as Pictorialism originated in England. In about 1890 a group led by Emerson broke away from the Royal Photographic Society to form what was to be known as the Linked Ring. His belief was that if photography was to hold a respected place in the arts, as the decorative arts were beginning to do with William Morris, it should set itself objectives and lay down 'rules' as to what constituted acceptable subjects. Many of these 'rules' were directly linked to Impressionism in Paris and the need for natural subjects. Atmospheric effects were achieved through manipulation of the print and, texture being of great importance, this period saw the use of carbon, platinum and gum bichromate in the printing process. Mallarmé's comment that 'to name an object is to suppress three-quarters of the enjoyment . . . suggestion, that is the dream,' though referring to poetry, became the slogan of the Pictorialists and such painters as Millet and Monet.

The revolution which took place was primarily against the standardization of the commercial world of photography. The group aimed to differentiate itself from the promoters of the snapshot, and it therefore emphasized the right of the unique single print, created in the studio, to be considered as a work of art, as opposed to the duplicatable snapshot. In Paris the greatest exponents of Pictorialism were Robert Demachy and Constant Puyo. Their work was associated with that of the 'Photo Club de Paris', which was created in 1894 in sympathy with the Linked Ring movement in London, and became known for advocating intervention by the photographer at both the negative and the print stages in order to achieve the desired effect. Through their work, to photograph became, once again, 'to draw or paint by light'.

Commandant Constant Puyo, founder of the 'Photo Club de Paris', was a moneyed member of the *haute bourgeoisie* and as such had no need to make a living from his work. He became one of the great chroniclers of bourgeois life in Paris at the turn of the century, primarily through his social position. His style can only be termed 'painterly', and like so many of his contemporaries his taste in subject-matter was for *fin-de-siècle* voluptuousness as much in his models as in his views. The draped nude, whether in the studio or outdoors, was a favourite subject, his aim being in the printing to soften the tones as one would in a drawing. In the context of the Pictorialism he promoted, his views of Paris should be seen less as representation than as impressions or symbolic evocations of a personal vision.

Demachy was better known than Puyo internationally, owing to his friendship with Alfred Stieglitz and through having his work published in Stieglitz's magazine *Camera Work* in New York during the latter's involvement with the Pictorialists. He became a great exponent of the gum bichromate technique, sometimes tinting the gum with ink or sanguine, and then working on the print with a paintbrush. He was to say of photography that the artistic merit of a photograph lay not so much in the way the image was captured as in the way it was subsequently transformed.

Another member of the Pictorialist movement was Edward Steichen. Though born in Europe he became a naturalized American and spent most of his life in the United States, becoming director of the photographic department at the Museum of Modern Art and mounting the celebrated exhibition 'The Family of Man' in 1955. He did, however, spend some time in Paris in 1900 at a crucial time in the development of the movement. An *habitué* of the *ateliers* he knew many of the artists and intellectuals of the turn of the century, and was instrumental in making the work of Cézanne and Matisse known across the Atlantic. At the time of his sojourn in Paris, Steichen was an excellent portraitist who found his models in the artistic circles in which he moved. He was particularly intent on photographing Rodin, and had read in New York of the scandal which had erupted on the unveiling of Rodin's sculpture of Balzac. He had a predilection for working in the half-light of dusk, and was later to photograph the statue of Balzac by moonlight. 'The Steeplechase' appeared in *Camera Work* in 1913 and illustrates well his aesthetic treatment of his subjects. It is a world apart from the style of either the amateur or the reporter. The image is intentionally grainy and contrasted, playing on the opposition of the

Maid
Puyo 1906

negative-positive. It captures all the style of the turn of the century, and more, through the technical rendering of the subject.

Only Pierre Dubreuil, who had been paying close attention to the gradual dissatisfaction of the Pictorialist style through Stieglitz's occasional visits to Paris, embraced a new subject-matter, that of the modern metropolis and the iconography it presented. Far removed from the formally composed photographs contained within the artist's framework, these were vibrant and isolated fragments seized on the run. It was Stieglitz who appropriated the term 'snapshots' for them – partly to get away from the more pretentious connotations of Pictorialism in which his interest soon waned; partly because it was exactly what they were and emphasized the objectivity of form that was to be the keynote of Secessionism, the movement which followed.

The desire of the Pictorialists had been to break away from the automatism of modern photography, and in particular from the amateur, but by the beginning of the twentieth century Pictorialism had effectively closed the door on itself, for there was only so much it could achieve. Stieglitz had been one of the first to become aware of this, and over the next few years its more active and progressive members were to move to New York and the Secessionist movement.

At the end of the first decade of the twentieth century Paris remained unrivalled for its charm and fashionable elegance despite its rapidly spreading suburbs and the industrialization taking place within the city walls. Lartigue, now in his late teens, was still obsessed by his photographic journal and deeply involved in the fashionable aspects of the city. He could on occasion be seen escorting elegantly dressed lady friends to such places as the skating ring at the Palais des Glaces, which was very much the rage. He also attended the Ballet at the Salle Garnier, where from 1908 onwards the Russian Ballet attracted much interest. Sergei Diaghilev was its director at the time, Nijinski its star, and Léon Bakst had become renowned for his scenery and costumes. The Paris music halls began to attract his attention as well, and when he wasn't photographing the people he was practising the 'Cake Walk', an American step which Maurice Chevalier had made famous in Paris.

Contrary to the conventions of Pictorialism, Lartigue took very few posed photographs or portraits, preferring the *instantané*. As a result, his work shows a freedom of expression and gesture rare in the photography of his day. Lartigue was the faithful representative of a class that was to lose many of its privileges after the First World War, but he captured the spirit of the city in its transition into the twentieth century better in some ways than the Pictorialists, for his evocative photographs were imbued with the city's spirit of romance and charm. It was in many ways a strange period for photography in Paris, for although the city had seen the medium through to maturity, and Pictorialism had proved that photography could be art, there was a feeling that it no longer knew where to turn for the regenerative spirit which it badly needed.

When Stieglitz opened his Little Gallery in New York on the evening of 25 November 1905, it was to mark an important moment for photography. Not only did it confirm the militant and elitist stance of the Photo-Secessionist group which Stieglitz controlled for the fifteen years of its existence from 1902, it also provided the guiding spirit for those who had to contend with the loss of direction that photography was experiencing in Paris. He had felt the growing need, since Pictorialism had become introspective and incestuous, to break away from tradition; and in particular to embrace the new ideas which were beginning to appear in artistic circles in Paris with the arrival of so many foreign artists. As with most breakaway movements, however, there was opposition to the new ideas, and in the years leading up to the war, photography in Paris stagnated in a cosy, well-established Pictorialism which had spread down the ranks to the photo clubs and amateur photographic societies.

In many ways, despite his geographical distance from Paris, Stieglitz acted as spokesman for its key figures who strove for a new freedom of expression in their need to redefine reality and allow a greater part to the subconscious. His gallery and the publication *Camera Work* provided an escape from the cul-de-sac in which Pictorialism found itself at the turn of the century, and Stieglitz became the central figure through his ability to attract and encourage creative talent, drawing to the ranks of the Secessionists such photographers as Alvin Langdon Coburn, Clarence H. White and Edward Steichen, who had all been active under the banner of Pictorialism. The Little Gallery, affectionately known as '291' from its address on Fifth Avenue, very rapidly became a refuge first for photographers and later for artists of many different disciplines who fled Paris. It was a spiritual haven and meeting-place for artists of both continents. In 1907 Stieglitz began to exhibit the work of the European *avant-garde*: Rodin, Cézanne, Picasso, Matisse, Picabia and Brancusi. Although the principal link with Paris remained Edward Steichen, who lived in Paris from 1908 until the war and acted as an intermediary or foreign correspondent for the '291', Stieglitz had also met the artists and became familiar with their work during his visits to Paris in 1907, 1909 and 1911. The exhibitions were innovative and full of the impact Stieglitz was seeking. The exhibition programme included African sculptures and drawings by Picasso and Braque, as well as photo-montages by Picabia and Duchamp. It was through these exhibitions and through the luxurious publication of his magazine from 1903 until 1917 that the *avant-garde* artists working in Paris found a public and that a new and more audacious vision appeared in the field of photography.

With the outbreak of the war in Europe, the photographers and artists who had found an audience for their work through Stieglitz came out to New York. Francis Picabia arrived in May 1915, shaking up the complacent public with his Dadaist principles. Marcel Duchamp followed and was to exhibit the now notorious urinal, entitled 'Fountain'. When Stieglitz's gallery closed owing to financial difficulties, the Modern Gallery with Stieglitz's moral and intellectual support and Picabia's financial assistance, continued to exhibit a range of art forms, from African art and photography, to the paintings of Picasso, Braque, Brancusi and Picabia. Without the support for their work in New York, many of these artists would never have had their extraordinary impact on the art world. After the war, however, the vision which Stieglitz had been nurturing was to find that its natural home was back in Paris, which is where it returned, stronger and clearer in its principles and having made a clean break with the past.

The construction of the Eiffel Tower, 14 October,
26 December 1888, 12 February, 31 March 1889
Anon. 1889

Eclipse
Atget 1911

Pont Alexandre III
Demachy 1900

A snapshot
Stieglitz 1911

Rue Eginhard
Atget *c.*1900

Nougat vendor
Atget *c.*1898

After the races, steeplechase day
Steichen 1913

Losers at the Auteuil races
Lartigue 1911

My cousin Bichonnade
Lartigue 1905

An out-of-the-ordinary bedroom, camping on the west wing
of Notre Dame, in order (not) to see Halley's comet
Gimpel 1910

Accident at the Gare Montparnasse
Anon. 1895

Avenue des Acacias
Lartigue 1912

Rue Saint-Rustique, Montmartre
Demachy 1900

Pont Alexandre III
Hachette *c.*1900

E. Canet
Atget *c.*1910

A l'Homme Armé
Atget *c.*1910

4 Rue du Jour
Atget 1908

*The great nave: wounded soldiers performing arms drill at the end
of their medical treatment, military hospital, Grand Palais*
Anon. 1914–16

Moonlight from the top of Notre Dame
Gimpel 1910

Fog, Avenue de l'Observatoire
Brassaï 1934

3

Carriage at the crossroads of Boulevards Montparnasse and Vavin
Brassaï 1932

By the beginning of the First World War photography had gained a prime position in both the artistic and scientific worlds. It had become the best way to record visual data from astronomical recordings to everyday events, and it was also accessible to the professional and the amateur alike. Despite the medium's problems of identity, with the coming of peace and the return of many artists and photographers excited by the victory of the Allied Forces, photography was to enjoy a period of revitalization.

The artistic world was also in full development, and nowhere more so than in Paris. Artists had been particularly eager, with the dawn of the new century, to start afresh rather than to inherit any of the old principles. Modigliani and Picasso were already vigorously challenging the old schools of thought. Picabia and Duchamp were the most controversial, with their Dadaist ideas, the main theme of which was the subordination of the artist's intention to the viewer's interpretation. Their innovative ideas produced such controversial work as Duchamp's 'ready-mades' and *objets trouvés*, which sought to find artistic definition in everyday objects by placing them within the context of a work of art.

At the outbreak of the war Picabia and Duchamp became involved with Stieglitz, who was still very much at the forefront of contemporary photography. It was through the exhibition of Picabia and Duchamp's work in New York, in which photographs were occasionally used in photo-collages and montages, that a renewed interest arose in photography. This had the effect of setting photography on to a new and unprecedented course, and its importance in the field of art became undeniable. There was a marriage of the photographic moment with the photographic object which suddenly brought photography to the forefront of artistic creativity. Paris was now more than ready to embrace this new vision.

Man Ray's name is probably the one most associated with the early regeneration of photography, and the way in which he came to photography from painting was typical of the time. His involvement with the medium was through direct collaboration with Duchamp and Picabia on his arrival in Paris in 1921. He had met both of them in New York through Stieglitz and had decided to follow them back to Paris at the end of the war. Through them he was very quickly introduced into French Surrealist circles, in particular to André Breton and Louis Aragon. Man Ray took a studio in the Rue Campagne Première, where Atget still had his *atelier*, and in order to support himself he found a job taking fashion photographs for Paul Poiret, a prominent designer of the time. His interest in the artistic potential of photography was relatively small, however, until one day he found he had placed an unexposed sheet of photographic paper in the developing tray by mistake. Instead of wasting it, he placed a number of objects on the sheet of paper and turned the light on. By stumbling upon what he was to call the Rayograph he had unwittingly rediscovered what Henry Fox Talbot had achieved all those years before with his photogenic drawings. The Surrealists, finding that the Rayograph was symbolic of the new vision in its breaking of the accepted rules, made much of his discovery. It was the first time a photograph could be considered a work of art without having captured an image through the lens.

With the end of the war the number of new artistic movements that sprung up throughout Europe and in particular in Eastern Europe was extraordinary. Dadaism had been the first to reassess our understanding of the artistic principles, and it was to spawn numerous movements which rapidly overshadowed it. Many of these new styles were related to the decorative arts, in particular to architecture, and in Paris everyone was talking about Le Corbusier and 'L'Esprit Nouveau'. It was a time dedicated to experimentation and trying anything that hadn't been done before. Most importantly it became the main method of communication to the public, and as such began to fulfil a major role in society.

Many of the artists who gravitated towards Paris in the early 1920s were seduced by the new medium and began to combine photography with other art forms, as the Dadaists had done. German and Russian Constructivism also acted as an enormous influence on intellectual and artistic thought throughout Europe at the time, and the artists' use of photography convinced people that it was the medium of the moment. It was accessible, relatively simple now as a process, and full of undiscovered potential. It was simplified even further by new technical advances such as the silent and smokeless flash and the wide-angle lens. The Russian Alexander Rodchenko and the Hungarian László Moholy-Nagy took up the Dadaist theme of 'constructing' works out of photographs, and after a visit to Paris in 1925 to see the World Fair of Modern Industry and the Decorative Arts, Moholy-Nagy in particular became instrumental in changing the course of photography. Moholy-Nagy had found himself at the forefront of the Russian Constructivist and Dada movements in Vienna before becoming, in 1923, the founding director of the Bauhaus photographic department in Weimar. On returning to Germany he not only began to include photography on the curricula of the art schools, he also collaborated on an exhibition of some one thousand photographs by European and American artists, entitled 'Film und Foto'. The exhibition set out to explain the medium and its place in the arts and, with a catalogue in three languages, it toured Germany, Austria and Switzerland, coming through Paris in 1929. Its impact on the world was undeniable and it confirmed the new position of respect that photography was to occupy at the forefront of the visual arts.

Paris, too, suddenly found itself the centre of attraction to a growing number of Americans eager to partake in the spirit of liberalism which had taken the city by storm. Many had come over as young recruits or as volunteers with the Red Cross towards the end of the war, but the period of Prohibition and the wave of puritanism which swept through the States in the 1920s brought over many more. Paris was an infinitely more liberal, artistic and intellectual *milieu* than New York, and offered a rich cultural atmosphere where painters, writers, musicians and dancers were able to flourish unimpeded by the moral restrictions so prevalent at home. Among those to whom Paris was kind and who will be eternally associated with the city are such names as James Joyce, T.S. Eliot, Gertrude Stein, Ezra Pound, Isadora Duncan, Henry James and Ernest Hemingway. While the United States was condemning publishers and artists on charges of obscenity, Paris delighted in its new-found glory and permissive ways. It became a melting-pot of artistic and literary talent which sought inspiration in the rich and exhilarating atmosphere of the city.

The stamping-ground of the expatriate writers, artists and journalists who were arriving in the city was the Boulevard Montparnasse and its cafés. Le Dôme, La Coupole, Le Select, La Rotonde, all grouped within a few metres of each other, became the heart and soul of the artistic and literary world, to which gravitated people of many different nationalities and artistic inclinations.

There was another element which sent Paris into a frenzy and made the atmosphere in the mid-1920s so memorable: the nightclubs. An American show, to be called *La Revue Nègre*, arrived in Paris in 1925 and immediately became the talk of the town. Its star, Josephine Baker, epitomized through her exuberance the influence of jazz and negro music which had taken the city by storm. Hemingway, after spending an evening dancing with her, described her as 'tall, café au lait skin, ebony eyes, paradise legs and a smile to forget all smiles'. Nightclubs opened all over Paris with names which would have been more at home in New Orleans, such as 'The Black Bottom' and 'The Shimmy'. Americanisms were now frequently heard, and it was *de rigueur* to use such words as *le cocktail* and *le jazz band*, and everyone, it appeared, was dancing *le Charleston*.

Hemingway's favourite club was 'Le Jockey', where Kiki de Montparnasse began her career as a singer. Sent to Paris at the age of fourteen by her mother to earn a living, she ended up in Montparnasse posing for painters and photographers, Man Ray and Brassaï among them. She had a fascinating face with a turned-up nose, and lank hair cropped like a boy's, as well as a voluptuous body. She exuded seductiveness and life. It was said of her skirt that 'it went up and down like a theatre curtain and that she raised immodesty to an art'. She was spontaneous and frank and symbolized Montparnasse's nonconformity more aptly than anyone. She became Man Ray's lover and later that of Fujita the Japanese artist.

In the same year that 'Les Années Folles' reached fever pitch with the arrival of *La Revue Nègre* and Josephine Baker, André Kertész left Budapest for Paris, a city he had long dreamed of coming to. He had spent thirteen years photographing in his native Hungary, taking time off whenever he could from his work at the stock exchange in order to photograph mostly rural scenes. Unlike many of the photographers working in Paris, he did not approach the medium via another discipline, and perhaps because he was essentially self-taught and instinctive, a deep sense of integrity underlies all his work. He considered himself an amateur throughout his career, denigrating the intellectual approach which was so prevalent among the photographers of the period.

One of the first things Kertész did on arrival in Paris in 1925 was to photograph scenes from his hotel window in the Rue Vavin. The metaphorical distancing element of working from the window suggests his reluctance to invade his subject-matter, and a preference for observing from afar. Kertész had an intimate and personal vision, with the freshness of someone looking at the city for the first time, but not without the deep melancholy and reserve of someone who is far from home.

As it happens, the solitary, vulnerable figure of the *émigré* wandering through the unfamiliar city, typified by Kertész during his early period, symbolized a general trend in photography. Paris was becoming a city of exiles, and the new photographic style reflected their situation. The city was being observed afresh through new cameras and photographers were looking at subjects which had not been considered before. In Kertész's obstinate desire to show the city as it really was, as much an aesthetic choice as an emotional one, he echoed loudly the documentary realist style of Atget, which up until then the public had largely chosen to ignore.

Kertész, despite his shyness, was excited by the explosion of interest in photography, and living only a few streets away from Montparnasse, soon found himself caught up in a social whirlwind. There was undoubtedly a feeling of freedom and exhilaration in the self-discovery of many foreign artists. It was the cafés which most epitomized the new exuberance, and the *émigrés* adopted these havens of conviviality as second homes. Kertész would almost certainly have heard of the Dôme while in Hungary, and just as his compatriots who preceded him had done, he made it the centre of his Parisian world. His friends, to begin with, were mostly Hungarians

living precariously but excited by their new adventure. Among them were Zilzer and Kassak, who were linked with the Expressionist movement, and Tihanyi, a deaf and dumb painter with whom he explored much of the city on first arriving. Through his Hungarian friends he was slowly introduced to other artists, who began to commission portraits from him for his engaging, natural and honest style. When his portraits began to earn him a small living he took a modest *atelier* at 5 Rue de Vanves, from the window of which he could see the Eiffel Tower.

Throughout his first year in Paris Kertész photographed the city whenever he could, and by 1926, through more deliberate framing, his street scenes had acquired a dynamism which replaced the melancholic vision of the early days. Kertész's Paris, though similar to Atget's in spirit, was not that of the 'Vieille Epoque', steeped in a sense of time passing: it was full of vitality and youth. A Paris of busy cafés, their terraces bulging with people, and of streets noisy with traffic and vibrating to the sound of the Métropolitain. When the bustle of the Montparnasse crossroads proved too much he would seek comfort from Montmartre, whose cobbled streets and many steep gradients and flights of steps reminded him of Old Budapest.

Avenue de l'Opéra
Kertész 1929

It became increasingly clear that photography was gaining renewed interest during the 1920s, and not only as a result of the work being done by the Constructivists and the Surrealists. Kertész and Brassaï, who became more popular as the decade wore on, were beginning to be associated with the photographer who had invented his own style three decades before. Even Atget himself, who had continued to photograph during the war despite the hardship he was to endure, now experienced a surge of popularity. Man Ray was living in the Rue Campagne Première, a few doors away from Atget's studio at No. 31, and was assisted at the time by Berenice Abbott. It would have been difficult not to notice Atget, older and poorer, still carrying his cumbersome antiquated camera and either showing his work to friends in his *atelier* or peddling his prints around the café terraces at the end of the street. In 1921 Atget had agreed to photograph the bordellos of Paris for a book on prostitutes. The book was never published, but it brought him into contact with artists such as Man Ray and Picasso, who began to pay him visits in his studio and occasionally bought prints from him. His coming into contact with the *avant-garde* did nothing, however, to change his style or to discourage him from continuing with the ambitious task he had set himself of capturing all that was artistic and picturesque in and around Paris. By 1926, when his wife died and he was at his most disillusioned, he had still never been published or exhibited.

Berenice Abbott, Man Ray's assistant and a photographer in her own right, was the first to spend some time looking at Atget's archives and to notice the remarkable purity of his work and the scope and integrity of his vision. She was greatly impressed by the extent of his documentation of the city, at the time amounting to some ten thousand plates and negatives. The same year, 1926, the Surrealists were to buy four prints from him for use in their magazine *La Révolution Surréaliste*, and his photograph of a group of people looking at an eclipse from the Place de la Bastille became the magazine's first cover. It was a belated and ironic recognition of his talent, since he not only belonged to a bygone age but was also far removed from Surrealism. His style became the great precursor of the social realist vogue which marked Paris so dramatically over the next decades. What interested the Surrealists was his photography's grounding in reality and its ability to convey the fantastic element in humdrum scenes of daily life. Atget, however, far from being concerned with the current debates on the status of photography, was simply pleased to sell his work.

Atget's approach to photography, which was rooted in an objective and humane vision intent on recording and preserving a social order which was rapidly disappearing, was to have far-reaching consequences. The element of authenticity in the recording of man's position in the changing world became the principal point of reference for all the photographers dedicated to a photo-journalistic style. Although the Surrealists' renewed interest in Atget and approval of his style may, restrospectively, be taken less seriously, since it was by their principles possible to reinterpret almost anything in order to give it new meaning, it should nevertheless be remembered that it was thanks to their approval of what he stood for that Atget became renowned. In August 1927, alone and destitute, Atget died, unaware of the legacy he was leaving.

The Rue Campagne Première, so close to the busy Montparnasse area which had become the locus of two fundamentally different but crucial styles in the development of photography, also became the home of another photographer who was to leave her charming mark on the city. It was through her work as a successful fashion model in New York that Lee Miller first became interested in working from the other side of the camera and heard of Man Ray. By this time, Man Ray had long since established himself among the Surrealists and now spent much of his time at the cafés with his friends who included Cocteau, Max Ernst, George Braque and Fernand Leger. His reputation had grown enormously and his work was attracting avid interest. Drawn to Paris by the wealth of artistic talent, Lee Miller arrived in 1929, the year of Salvador Dali's first major exhibition, with a letter of introduction to Man Ray from Edward Steichen. She sought him out on her very first day in Paris and announced herself as his pupil. On being told dismissively that he did not take pupils and that in any case he was going away on holiday, she declared that she was going with him. They spent the next three years of their lives together, very much in love with one another and collaborating closely in their work. She became Man Ray's favourite model, and he taught her everything he knew about photography. She very rapidly assimilated the Surrealist vision into her own work and she began to mix with Man Ray's friends. Their relationship was such a close and intense one that Miller would often carry out Man Ray's commissions when he had more work than he could manage.

Their collaboration is probably best remembered for the reinvention of the solarized photograph which, like the Rayograph a few years before, became an important feature in the Surrealist movement. The story goes that Miller and Man Ray were in the darkroom when Miller felt something crawl across her foot. Letting out a yell she switched on the light, accidentally further exposing areas of the negative and creating a partial reversal of tones. Man Ray kept the technique a secret until his liaison with Miller ended in 1932. Both Man Ray and Miller were to use the solarization effect to their advantage, yet Lee Miller's style remained highly individualistic and not at all derivative of her mentor's. She had a powerful ability to see what was arresting in everyday situations, and she used the camera to reframe an otherwise ordinary vision, such as a café chair or a shop awning, and turning it into something new and esoteric. The result is both refreshing and strong, jolting the viewer into looking at things differently. She very quickly became an enchanting figure in Parisian café society. Beautiful, intelligent and highly creative, she was the subject of many Surrealist photographs, and her charismatic nature often made her the centre of attraction at the terraces of the cafés. Picasso and Paul Eluard became lifelong friends of hers, and although she left Man Ray to move to Egypt with her new lover Aziz Eloui Bey, she returned during the war to continue her work as a photographer, this time as a photo-journalist.

In 1927, a certain Lucien Vogel walked into an exhibition that had been arranged for Kertész at the Sacre du Printemps, a small gallery which had started to show photography. What he saw immediately moved him to invite Kertész to collaborate on a magazine he was about to launch called *Vu*. The magazine became the mainstay of Kertész's commercial career as well as that of most of the great photographers working in Paris at the time. After the war, especially in Germany, there was a surge in the publication of news and current affairs magazines, which chose to do large print runs in order to bring down their production costs. They had an enormously wide readership and aimed to distract the reader with articles of human interest and the occasional serialization of a popular novel. They used photography in a way in which it had never been used before, relying on uniformity and strength of style to capture the interest of its public. The photographs published were essentially photo-essays based on sequence and a strong sense of graphic layout. Photographers were credited and as a result some of them became household names.

For people like Kertész, and later Brassaï, the magazines provided an immediate and powerful outlet for their style of photography. By 1936 every one of *Vu*'s regular contributors was included in the International Exhibition of Contemporary Photography. Over a period of ten years *Vu* and a similar magazine called *Art et Médecine* became the most extraordinary show-case not only of the best photography in Paris, but also of the city in all its glory. The October 1932 issue of *Vu* was dedicated specifically to Paris and included work by Brassaï, Kertész, Germaine Krull and Maurice Tabard, as well as articles by Cocteau and Pierre Mac Orlan, the photographic critic. As early as 1928 the latter was to say of photography that 'the art

Louvre and Tuileries Kertész 1931

may be divided into two classes . . . plastic photography and documentary photography. The second is akin to literature and is nothing other than the observation of contemporary life apprehended at the right moment by an artist capable of seizing it.' His comment already contained the germ of Henri Cartier-Bresson's slogan 'the decisive moment' a decade later.

Soon after his arrival in Paris, Kertész had contributed to such magazines as the *Berliner Illustrierte* and the *Münicher Illustrierte Presse*, covering subjects of cultural interest such as the Eiffel Tower's fortieth anniversary, but it was with *Vu* that Kertész enjoyed the closest and most rewarding collaboration.

With the advent of the illustrated press the city of Paris took on a new role. The movement, which became known as L'Ecole de Paris, and which had grown from the Surrealist doctrine that a work of art should arise out of the unforeseen and the unplanned, together with the new breed of photographers who stalked the streets of Paris for that decisive moment, compounded to make the city the new protagonist. A whole genre of documentary photography specifically related to Paris was born, to the extent that in 1929 Kertész was asked to illustrate the biography of a Hungarian poet with views of Paris. The search for the very essence of the city soon became the driving motivation of many photographers.

It was another Hungarian photographer, however, who was to capture the darker side of the city with a technique of photographing at night which became his trademark. When Brassaï, who took his name from his birthplace of Brasso in Transylvania, arrived in Paris in 1924 from Hungary, he had no intention of taking up photography. He had sworn himself to his love of painting, and before long he was on intimate terms with Picasso and Giacometti and was well known in all the studios around Montparnasse. It was only towards the end of the decade, through his exploration of the city at night with his friend Kertész, who was also renting rooms at the Hôtel des Terrasses at the time, that he decided it was the only medium that could capture the *demi-monde* that so delighted him. He came to know Paris so intimately that Henry Miller called him the 'Eye of Paris', for he sought out every last cul-de-sac of the city and knew every backstreet. Although he would be best known for the photographs he took at night, he also worked for many of the Surrealist painters. He became a close friend of Picasso through photographing his work and his *atelier*, and was introduced to the central figures of the Surrealist movement such as Skira, Breton, Eluard and Dali.

As Brassaï's technique revealed, the notion of 'witnessing' became important again in photographic circles, and through the illustrated press the power of photography slowly made itself felt. With the introduction of new techniques and more manageable cameras, in particular the Leica, a new facet of Paris was emerging; a more marginal or individual side was being shown by photographers who found themselves enticed into the very bowels of the city in search of its secret soul. Night photography was not in fact a new discovery. Nadar in 1860 had photographed the catacombs of Paris by using a magnesium flash, but Kertész and Brassaï's work was different. They did not work by flashlight but rather by long exposure, relying entirely on the available light. The result was a highlighting of certain areas of the image, contrasted with areas of darkness. The effect is surreal, producing a twilight world of sinister beauty. The city at night became, through their lenses, not merely the opposite of a daylight image, but a Paris transformed into a world of eerie shadows, haloes and reflections.

When Brassaï was not wandering the city with Kertész, he was often accompanied by Henry Miller, who sought the same subject-matter for his novels. They spent much of their time walking in the XIIIe and XIVe *arrondissements*, entering delapidated houses and exploring streets which most people avoided at night on account of their unsalubrious aspect. What they found was Paris at its most raw and most authentic. The folklore of the city which had been kept alive by cover of night since the previous century was suddenly revived. They were obliged to use cunning to obtain access to the bars and areas they wished to explore. Crime was still high and it was not uncommon for Brassaï to be threatened by an angry pimp. On one occasion at the Quatre Saisons, a *bal musette* on the Rue de Lappe, he was robbed of all the photographic plates which he had just exposed of the dancing couples.

The street fairs were also a favourite with Brassaï, who enjoyed the noise of the rollercoasters and the smell of gunpowder from the fireworks and the shooting stalls. He was also able, through astute pleading and the inevitable bribe, to gain access to Notre Dame and to climb the 378 steps to the very top. Here he was so enchanted by what he saw that he inadvertently stepped on a dead pigeon, still warm, and the moment was fixed for ever in his mind as well as on film. Brassaï even spent an evening with the cesspool cleaners who, in the early 1930s, were still obliged to drain the pits 'manually'. Only some of the smarter areas had benefited from the new sewers installed during the Second Empire, making the cesspool cleaners a familiar but unwelcome sight in the east of Paris between the hours of midnight and six o'clock in the morning. Brassaï was also an *habitué* of the banks of the Seine, where he would stop occasionally to share a bottle of *pinard*, or cheap wine, with the tramps.

Brassaï is probably best remembered for his coverage of the city's prostitutes and the more lugubrious *bals musettes* and *pissotières*. Paris has never really had a red-light district as such, although there have always been *quartiers chauds*, or hot spots. In those days every area had its quota of brothels, each catering to a different social class. Montparnasse and St Germain had the largest number of them, with as many as five in the Rue Mazarine alone. The more extravagant of these houses were situated near the Opéra and Palais Royal, but the large marketplace of Les Halles was another such *quartier chaud*, which Brassaï covered extensively, getting to know many of the girls and the hotels, known as *maisons d'illusion*, where they were allowed by law to take their customers, but not to live. Les Halles was an area frequented by the farmers who came into Paris for the market. More often than not, having delivered their produce, they would spend the remaining part of the night drinking and enjoying the company of the girls, before hurrying back to their farms at dawn. The extraordinary glass and steel pavilions which made up the market were built by Baltard in 1856. It remained a thriving centre of commerce until it was razed in 1971 to make way for the modern complex of steel and concrete that we know today.

The *bals musettes* took their name from the wind instrument similar to the Breton bagpipes. They were popular dance halls, on the lines of La Grande Chaumière in Montparnasse at the turn of the century, and tended to be frequented by sailors and the servant girls working for the bourgeois families in the *quartiers chics* of Paris. By the time Brassaï photographed them, the *musette* had been replaced by the accordion and they were more likely to be the haunts of pimps. The Rue de Lappe, near the Bastille, had a particularly high number of *bals musettes*, each one catering for a different clientèle.

The *pissotières*, or urinals, sometimes also called *vespasiennes* after the Emperor Vespasian in the first century, are particularly noticeable by their frequent presence in Brassaï's photographs. Unlike most cities, where they tend to be hidden away from the public gaze, Paris had no qualms in erecting them in the open, often in the middle of public squares. Most date from the early nineteenth century, and in 1930 there were some thirteen hundred scattered throughout the city. They very rapidly became haunts for homosexual pick-ups, and many famous figures of Parisian society were caught by the police and fined the customary one thousand francs. In order to put a stop to this practice, the municipal council slowly had most of them removed, but not before they were immortalized by Brassaï, as well as by Proust and Henry Miller in their novels.

Brassaï's nocturnal perambulations produced *Paris by Night* in 1932. His great ability to play with direct and indirect light created a highly atmospheric world; at times conveying an interpretation of reality which unsettled the viewer. Sights that we are used to seeing are represented to us in their new and unfamiliar guise in the night. The statue in the Luxembourg Gardens seen through the gates, symbolically inviting us into a new realm, is no longer the dark silhouette against a daylight background that we expect it to be, but a white and ghostlike shape against the dark backdrop of the night. As with Kertész, Brassaï's work was appropriated by the Surrealist movement for its ability to capture the 'fantastic' in what has been rendered banal through habit. He was able to portray an anonymous side of Paris which was a great departure from the more formal and public photographs being taken in the Second Empire. He had an unprecedented ability to make the ordinary unforgettable, and to find the sensational in everyday life.

Another foreign photographer who was able to localize the evocative and suggestive detail of the city was Ilse Bing, who came to Paris from Germany in 1930. Like so many expatriate photographers, she revealed her love for the city through the candid spontaneity of her photographs. She did not, on her arrival, seek out the photographers she had heard so much about, but tried instead to support herself with various jobs for the German illustrated press. She covered an eclectic array of subjects for them, such as the Can-Can dancers at the *Folies Bergère*, the Moulin

Rouge, and a Couture ball at the Opéra. She lived for a short period at the Hôtel de Londres in the Rue Bonaparte, walking the streets with her Leica and becoming a familiar face at the small exhibition openings at La Pléïade in the Boulevard Raspail.

Old photographer's studio, Boulevard Montparnasse
Bing 1933

Ilse Bing very rapidly made a reputation for herself with her photographs, which, like those of Kertész and Brassaï, were labelled 'documentary humanism'. She was known also as the 'Queen of the Leica', which she had taken up in 1929, a few years after Leitz, the German optical firm, had brought it on to the market. She was to say that it was for her 'an extension of my eye, going wherever I go, enabling me to convey things in a more solitary way'. Emmanuel Sougez, a critic and photographer and founding editor of *L'Illustration*, encouraged her to submit her prints to Julien Levy for his New York exhibition 'Modern European Photography' in 1932. Levy was a renowned dealer and curator in New York who followed closely the developments in photography in Europe and who was particularly interested in the work being produced in Paris. Ilse Bing found herself next to Kertész, Man Ray and Brassaï, as well as Germaine Krull who had come from Germany in 1924, as epitomizing the new style. The exhibition was a landmark in the history of photography in Paris, for it confirmed the position these photographers had achieved on the international scene.

Surrealism was still very much in evidence in Paris, with the publication in 1933 of the magazine *Le Minotaure*, for which Picasso did the first cover and Dali and Eluard provided illustrations. Although Ilse Bing's style was undeniably Surrealist in its attention to the simple details in life, it had a poetic and intimate dimension rarely seen in the Surrealists' work. She, too, eventually became caught up by the whirlwind of Montparnasse and moved to lodgings in the Boulevard Raspail, where she was able to set up a darkroom in her kitchen. Her photographs of the city conveyed the very edge of reality, the truth of the captured instant in which, like Kertész, she attempted to examine the nature of things and their relationship to the universe. When Man Ray relinquished his exclusivity on the solarization process in 1934, it was taken up by a number of photographers, including Maurice Tabard, who began using it in his fashion photographs. Ilse Bing also took it up, giving some of her work an added dream-like quality. She enjoyed unexpected juxtapositions in her photographs and often included street signs and posters in her compositions. Like Brassaï, she had a particular fascination for photographing the effects of light, and created a whole series of photographs based on street lights or their reflection on water.

As the decade advanced with news of the civil war in Spain and the growing fascism in Italy, photography in Paris could be clearly divided into two camps: 'Those that looked outward to the realities that surrounded them and would eventually threaten them, and those that looked within the medium and their inspiration for an aesthetic solution to the changes in the world.' Lee Miller, who had enjoyed a flourishing artistic career with Man Ray in the early 1920s, was to return to Paris during the war as a photo-journalist with strong moral and political convictions. Bill Brandt, who had also spent time with Man Ray in Paris, was more interested, on his return to England, in the social documentation of the coal miners and the poor. As Europe became more unsettled there was a very evident shift away from the artistic innovations of the Surrealists towards a documentary humanism, where the photographer became social observer. The whole language of photography was evolving, now preferring words such as 'seize' and 'capture', or talking of 'an impulse to appropriate'. Even Man Ray, writing in 1934 in an introduction to a retrospective book, felt the need to defend his preoccupation with individual emotion rather than the social or the moral.

As early as 1933, when Hitler was made Chancellor of the Reich, many people began to feel uncomfortable in their native Germany. Fritz Lang moved to Paris to escape the harassment he was being subjected to. Marlene Dietrich came over to sing at the Ange Bleu to the many expatriates anxious about the changing times. The city was also by then well established as a centre for photography. Exhibitions, talks and events on photography were being held regularly; new galleries such as L'Escalier or the Plume d'Or were concentrating exclusively on photography and exhibiting the new style which Paris found itself witness to. Photography was full of innovation and, owing to the large proportion of foreigners, new influences proliferated.

One influence however, was far from being foreign. It was that of Henri Cartier-Bresson, who in 1932 gave up painting, which he had been studying under André Lohte, to take up photography. Such was the power of his photographs that within a year he had been asked by Julien Levy to exhibit in his gallery in New York. In Paris his compositions were being praised not only for their extraordinary beauty but also for their rigorous harmony and balance of form, which later inspired a whole generation of photographers to turn to photo-journalism. Although his early period produced a body of work which had an enormous impact on photography, it was during his time as a photo-journalist with Magnum that he would make the greatest impact. The importance of Cartier-Bresson at this stage, however, lay in the vital role he played in bringing the two extremes of photography, the artistic and the documentary, together into what became known as 'modern photography'. Cartier-Bresson's photographs offered both a rich narrative content and a purity of form which bridged the gap between the two camps and brought photography into a new era.

The term which more than any other confirmed the change photography had undergone in the last twenty years was 'photo-journalism', which had become synonymous with the documentary, realist style which so many photographers were adopting. The photographer who impressed on the world the non-artistic role that the style was to have was Robert Capa. Ironically it was Louis Aragon, the Surrealist poet turned political activist, who was instrumental in laying the foundations for the new style of photo-journalism when he founded a Communist newspaper called *Ce Soir* and invited Capa and Henri Cartier-Bresson to collaborate with him. Robert Capa who arrived from Berlin where he had been making a clear political stance against fascism, always maintained that he was a journalist and was for the most part unconcerned with photographic theory. But by the time he came back from the Spanish Civil War, *Picture Post* magazine in England had published eleven pages of Capa's photographs, preceded by a full-page portrait of him with a credit which read: 'The Greatest War Photographer in the World'.

By 1935 military service was extended to twenty-four months as fears of war increased. Lee Miller, on returning to the city towards the end of 1937, attended a Surrealist ball given by the Rochas sisters. Many of her old friends were present, including Man Ray and Paul Eluard, with whom she renewed her friendship. But the political unrest in the city accelerated over the next year and it wasn't long before they were forced to move to the south of France. The Hôtel Vaste Horizon in Mougins, where Picasso and Dora Maar were living and where Man Ray decided to spend the summer with his Martiniquaise girlfriend, became the group's new base. As they were leaving, thousands of soldiers were gathering at the Gare du Nord and the Gare de l'Est, singing songs by Edith Piaf and Tino Rossi as they waited to catch the trains which would take them to the front. Ilse Bing and her husband were interned shortly afterwards in separate concentration camps. She was more fortunate than many in her position, however, for her internment lasted only ten weeks. But she had to spend nine months in Marseilles waiting for the emigration papers which would allow her to leave for the United States. Despite the wait, her work, which was sent on by a friend in Paris, arrived after her departure and remained in a warehouse until after the war. She was finally able to retrieve it, but not before the US Customs had appropriated a great many negatives because she was unable to pay the high import levy.

Few photographers were to remain in Paris during the war, most having fled to New York or the south of France, and it wasn't until the liberation four years later that the key figures of the movement would reappear on the scene. By the time they returned, Paris would be a very different city.

Eiffel Tower
Kertész 1925

The Pont Neuf on a rainy day
Kertész 1931

The steps of Montmartre
Kertész 1925–7

Champs Elysées
Kertész 1927–9

Stairwell, Montparnasse
Kertész 1928

Lamplighter at dusk, Place de la Concorde
Brassaï *c.*1933

Rue de la Verrerie
René-Jacques 1932

Corner of the Rue de la Charbonnière and Rue de Chartres
René-Jacques 1936

Anglers behind Notre Dame
Kertész 1925

Quai Saint-Bernard
Cartier-Bresson 1932

Ice-cream vendor, XVIIᵉ arrondissement
Boubat 1954

Rue des Ursins
Kertész 1929–31

Electric storm
Kertész c.1926

Pont des Arts through the clock of the Institut de France
Kertész 1929–32

Place Vendôme, in front of Schiaparelli
Schall 1937

Guerlain
Miller 1930

Pont Alexandre III
Klein 1960

4

THE MAGNUM STYLE & PHOTO-JOURNALISM

1939 ▶ 1968

The painter of the Eiffel Tower
Riboud 1953

The position in which photography found itself at the outbreak of the Second World War was summed up very precisely by Ernst Haas, a friend and collaborator of Robert Capa and Cartier-Bresson who later joined Magnum: 'There are two types of photographers in the world: those who make photographs and those who take photographs. The first have their studios and for the others their studio is the world.' The war had taken the photo-journalists far afield, and they found that their work would continue to do so more and more in the years to come. Paris nonetheless remained the home base to which these photographers returned after assignments and from which they continued to draw inspiration.

The term photo-journalist had first come into use in 1937 when *Life* magazine was created. It was to stand for a new breed of photographers who were to travel to all four corners of the world and fascinate a rapidly growing public by the images they brought back. Photo-journalists would need to be capable not only of capturing that 'decisive moment' of action, but also of making an assessment, through their own ideas, convictions and frame of reference, of the situation with which they were confronted and which they had to convey to the public. There were three principal factors which enabled the forceful new style to become firmly established in Paris: the presence of two magazines, *Regards* and *Paris Match*, both of which were intent on emulating *Life*; the Magnum agency, which was to make of photo-journalism almost a myth; and two of its photographers in particular, Robert Capa and Henri Cartier-Bresson, who, from the movement's beginnings through to its heyday, were to be its spiritual, artistic and moral leaders.

Ideas such as the one behind the founding of Magnum, which didn't take place until well after the war, take time to mature and even longer to put into practice. The catalytic meeting between two of the protagonists occurred on a bus between Montmartre and Montparnasse on a cold day in January 1934. Henri Cartier-Bresson, tall and elegantly dressed, probably on his way to the Dôme after one of his frequent trips abroad, was adjusting the lens on his Leica. The other person, hunched and wearing thick spectacles and much less elegantly attired, was David Seymour (born Szymin) but known to everyone as Chim. Fascinated by the camera, he engaged Cartier-Bresson in conversation. Had it not been for the latter's Leica, the two might never have met.

A few weeks later, at the Dôme where Hemingway was telling stories of the Pamploma Fiera and Henry Miller was dining with Anaïs Nin, Chim introduced Cartier-Bresson to André Friedmann, later known as Robert Capa. The two could not have been more different, either in nature or background. Capa was gregarious and reactionary; Cartier-Bresson was reserved and aristocratic. Together with Chim they would have made an unlikely trio, but their friendship and later collaboration was to last until the untimely deaths of Capa and Chim some twenty years later.

Of the two, it was Henri Cartier-Bresson who approached photography from the point of view of an artist. The product of an expensive education, he was highly precocious for his age. By the time he left school he had read all the great literary works, was well versed in the history of art, and had decided to take tuition in painting. He found, however, that he was too restless in his desire to discover life to spend much time at the easel, preferring to spend it in the company of André Breton and his friends at the Montparnasse cafés. He flirted with Surrealism for a while and then discovered the camera with which his name was to be associated for evermore, the Leica. When Chim met him on the bus to Montparnasse, Cartier-Bresson had already taken some of his most famous images. Few were of Paris, however, for there was too much going on in the world for him to be able to stay in the same place for long. It was not until 1936, when he became a photo-journalist for Aragon's pro-Communist *Ce Soir* newspaper, and went on assignments to Spain and Italy, that his work became more widely known. The Leica became his travelling companion and his surrogate eye during the many trips he was to make to the Far East and Third World countries which were undergoing such dramatic change. He, like Kertész, made the most of whatever chance sent his way, and his early work exudes spontaneity and a dramatic sense of graphic impact. He always tried to 'line up the mind, the eye and the heart' in his photographs, and, owing to his wealth of intellectual and artistic knowledge, no one was better able to achieve this. Julien Levy exhibited him in New York as early as 1933 and went to great lengths to explain, in a text accompanying the exhibition, what Cartier-Bresson's work was about, fearing that many might not understand it. 'Call it equivocal,' he said, 'ambivalent, anti-plastic or accidental photography.' His work encapsulated everything that photography over the next two decades would aspire to. It was a style that could re-evaluate and document the rapidly changing world. His approach was rigorous: he would never, for example, re-frame an image after it had been taken, and he was known to view photographs upside-down to see whether they stood the test of form and composition.

As for Capa, exiled from Hungary for political activities and chased out of Germany by Nazism, he arrived in Paris in 1936 as André Friedmann, changed his name to Robert Capa, and went to fight alongside the Spanish Republican forces during the Civil War. In Hungarian the word *capa* means 'sword', an apt choice for a war correspondent and particularly revealing of his personality. He was still only twenty-three years old, impetuous, spirited and dedicated to his political beliefs. His first memorable image was of Trotsky in Denmark in 1931, and his last was of soldiers walking beside him in Cambodia, taken inadvertently as the mine that killed him exploded. He was not happy unless he was in the thick of battle. He would say that if a photograph was bad it was because he hadn't got close enough to the action. After the Spanish Civil War, when his image of the falling soldier brought him worldwide fame, he found himself on the frontlines of another war, this time in China in 1938. From there, on assignment for *Life* magazine and *Ce Soir*, he wrote of his idea of creating in Europe 'with Cartier and Chim' an organization 'which would in no way resemble an ordinary agency'.

Over the next few years Capa was to find himself on the frontlines of most of the battles the world was witness to. The public's knowledge of the war in Africa owed much to Capa's presence there and the photographs he took. With his uncanny sixth sense for being at the right place at the right time, he was also present on D-Day with the First Division on Omaha Beach. It was believed that he had been killed during the landing, until he turned up in a hospital ship clutching the all-important rolls of film.

To Capa's great distress, when the film was rushed to the Time Life offices for processing, the printer, overawed by the importance of his task, bathed the negatives in hot water by mistake, thereby ruining most of the exposures. When *Life* ran the pictures, the editors tried to explain away the hazy quality by saying that Capa in the heat of battle had shot the film slightly out of focus. Later, when Capa came to write his autobiography he called it, bitterly, *Slightly out of Focus.*

A nomad for most of his working life, Capa roamed the world, paying little heed to conventional considerations. He claimed Paris as his home, however, and would always return to it after his assignments.

Both Capa and Cartier-Bresson were strongly influenced by Kertész. He was their poetic source and had the visual eloquence which has so often been described as the photographic equivalent of rhyme and rhythm. Through their numerous war assignments they were inspired by Kertész to make their photography incisive and informative. Despite that overriding influence and the appearance of a homogenous

A French Resistance fighter pushes a German prisoner through the streets of the liberated city
Capa 1944

style, however, the temperaments of the two photographers were radically different. Capa's prime motivation was as a participant in the event, not as an observer. What he founded was not so much a style of photography as a breed of photographers for whom courage and risk were the mark of a truer photography. Cartier-Bresson, on the other hand, was the distanced observer *par excellence*, with a control of space and time which permitted him to focus on unexpected juxtapositions. He constructed his images architecturally; Capa took them as they came. If Cartier-Bresson was imagination itself, Capa was impulse. What they had in common above all was an extraordinary instinct for photographic impact through composition, which was so characteristic of the style which became associated with photo-journalism in general and Magnum in particular.

On 23 August 1944, the French Second Armoured Division received instructions from General Leclerc that they were to spearhead the Allied entry into Paris. It became known during the course of the day that they would be taking the N20 Orléans to Paris road from Arpajon, but also that only French journalists would be allowed to accompany the Division. Capa, undeterred, got hold of a jeep and driver and caught up with Leclerc's rearguard on the morning of 25 August. Weaving in and out of the French tanks, they were soon just one vehicle away from the armoured car in which Leclerc stood. To the best of their knowledge Capa and his colleague were the first Americans to enter Paris, passing through the Porte d'Orléans at exactly 9.40 a.m., directly behind Leclerc. The German resistance to the approach was minimal. Only a few sharpshooters remained, creating the occasional disturbance, such as when the procession reached the Hôtel de Ville and found itself under fire from a group of

German snipers hiding on the roof of the building. The main impediment was the crowd which had gathered in hundreds of thousands to welcome home the troops. In the afternoon Capa was back on the bonnet of his jeep in de Gaulle's triumphant procession from the Arc de Triomphe to Notre Dame, photographing the euphoric crowds. That evening Capa visited his old haunts around Montparnasse and St Germain and began to prepare a temporary office for the many Time Inc. correspondents who were arriving in Paris. This was at the Hôtel Scribe, near the Opéra, which already housed the headquarters of the Allied press.

Hemingway, no doubt to Capa's great irritation, always maintained that he had reached Paris before General Leclerc's troops and, heading straight for the Ritz, had liberated it single-handed. The international hotels in Paris at the end of the war were the only sources of drink and cigarettes. Most had limitless supplies of champagne, and none more so than the Ritz. Capa came to join Hemingway at the Ritz on the evening of the Liberation to catch up on events since they had parted company at the Mont Saint Michel after the Allied landing. At a nearby table probably would have been Coco Chanel, who moved permanently into a suite at the hotel in 1934, remaining there throughout the Occupation and until her death in 1971. F. Scott Fitzgerald, Cole Porter, Marlene Dietrich and King Alfonso of Spain were all regular guests, and the hotel was Churchill's headquarters on his visits to the city after 1944. Proust, too, was a great *habitué* of the bar at the Ritz, and when he became bedridden he continued to send his chauffeur the few blocks from his apartment to collect the daily bottle of beer which was kept for him in the refrigerator.

Lee Miller, like Capa and Hemingway, also arrived in Paris on Liberation Day. She had been working for *Vogue* in London since the outbreak of the war, covering the Blitz and writing an occasional fashion story for them. Her reaction to the war had led her to a more courageous and aggressive style of photography, yet without any dilution of the spontaneity of her early images. Aware of the boom the illustrated press was going through, with magazines such as *Life*, *Look* and *Fortune* producing regular high-quality photo stories, she applied in 1941 for accreditation as a correspondent to the US War Department. Through her work on the Blitz she became a highly respected photo-journalist and would photograph alongside many of the greatest of them, covering more and more stories for *Vogue*, for which she did both the writing and photographing. Not long before her arrival in Paris on Liberation Day, she had witnessed the almost entire destruction of St Malo as the US 83rd Division recaptured the town. In her inimitable style she photographed the whole ordeal from the honeymoon suite she was occupying.

Air raid
Lartigue 1944

When she arrived in the capital, she was to write: 'Paris had gone mad. The long graceful dignified avenues were invaded with flags and filled with screaming, cheering people. Girls, bicycles, kisses and wine, and around the corner sniping, a bursting grenade and a burning tank. The bullet holes in the windows were like jewels, the barbed wire in the boulevards add a new decoration . . . I arrived exhausted by my share of millions of handshakes, handshakes for the *femme soldat*.'

Lartigue had already returned to Paris by the time the Allies liberated the city.

He had been living in a garret in the Rue Desbordes-Valmore since 1943, when the city was still a target for bombing raids. He documented these in the way he would have photographed an air display – for himself – for he was still an avid photographer but seemed oblivious to any professional or academic interest in the subject. On Liberation Day, as Capa drove in through the Porte d'Orléans, Lartigue was photographing his companion among the waiting crowds in the Place Blanche. The tricolour flag which flew from their top floor window was the largest in the square and reached right down to the pavement.

With Paris liberated, Capa felt he was home again. When the Hôtel Scribe became too noisy and crowded with the numerous Time Inc. journalists who had converged on Paris, Capa moved his personal operations to the Lancaster, a quiet hotel near the Champs Elysées which had been put at his disposal. The focus of attention in Paris in the first few weeks after the city's liberation shifted to the large hotels in the areas around the Place de la Concorde, the Opéra and the Champs Elysées. Among the various groups of reporters, photo-journalists and army officials who took over these hotels, Capa, with his unfailing energy, was at the very centre of the frenzy which gripped the city. On VE Day, Capa was on the roof of one of the buildings around the Opéra, photographing the crowds surging below in a state of intoxication at their new-found freedom. With his passion for helping photographers and his acute business sense, he was always on the lookout for a lucrative deal which would benefit him or his colleagues. To overcome their transportation problems, he arranged for cars to be bought on the black market. He put John Morris, recently arrived from London to run the *Life* operations, in touch with Cartier-Bresson, who had been covering the work of the Resistance. He never missed out on a deal, and somehow always found the money in time. A favourite Capa story tells how once, when he was unable to pay Pierre Gassmann, the printer who later handled Magnum's archives, he borrowed money from him which he successfully gambled at the races and so paid off his debt.

Pierre Gassmann, who had left his native Germany in horror at the advance of Nazism, became a key element in the growth of photo-journalism in Paris. Gassmann could scarcely have avoided the call of printing had he wanted to, since his mother was a radiographer and he had grown up with the smells of fixing fluid and developer in the house. By the age of thirteen he was developing 30 × 40cm X-ray prints and already had an extraordinary aptitude for reading negatives and seeing the world back to front. His mother became something of a celebrity through her work, and entertained such members of the Bauhaus as Paul Klee and Moholy-Nagy, to whom Gassmann showed his first photographs. After studying law in Berlin, he decided to move to Paris, drawn by the magical names of Man Ray, Brassaï and Kertész, whom he greatly admired and whose work made him feel that he already knew the city. One evening at the Dôme in Montparnasse he met Chim and Cartier-Bresson as well as Gisèle Freund, who had also come to Paris to make a living from photography. In 1935 he discovered to his amazement that he was living in the same building as Brassaï. It took Gassmann three months to find the courage to show him his photographs of Paris, but through Brassaï he eventually met Kertész and found himself integrated into the expatriate community, together with other German photographers such as Erwin Blumenfeld and Philippe Halsman.

At the end of the war Gassmann set up a darkroom in his bathroom and began to work as a freelance reporter. It was due to Capa, however, that he realized that his skills lay more in the darkroom than on the battlefield with his camera, and was persuaded to become Magnum's official printer. In 1950 he founded Pictorial Service in the Rue de la Comète, and it has been an institution in photography in Paris ever since. Gassmann was able to print the work of Magnum's photographers with great intuition and understanding, interpreting the negative rather than just copying from it. He was asked by the city of Paris to reprint Atget's negatives and also printed the work of most of the great photographers who have photographed the city.

Unlike the First World War, after which photography had been left ailing and directionless, the end of the Second World War saw the medium receive a massive boost. Thanks to Capa, and the force and presence with which he entered the city on its Liberation Day, photography was now elevated to its primary function of documenting the world for those who could not witness it at first hand. It bathed in a newfound glory and prestige which, with Magnum as its spearhead, it was to retain for the next few decades. As for Cartier-Bresson, it would be wrong to say that he had instigated a school of photography, for he never took kindly to the adulation of his work and he certainly never taught. Yet his style, together with Capa's, became an institution and a source of inspiration for a whole generation.

Post-war Paris rapidly regained its former *joie de vivre* and exuberance. Now, however, it was to the cafés around St Germain that people returning after the war tended to gravitate. Less Bohemian than Montparnasse, St Germain and in particular the Café Flore became the new fashionable and intellectual centre. In 1946 the mood was reinforced when Christian Dior's 'New Look' burst on to the streets of Paris. With their narrow waists and mid-length ample skirts, his fashions caught everyone's imagination.

The Ritz enters the story again in June 1945, when Capa, on hearing that Ingrid Bergman was staying there en route to Germany, to entertain the US troops, decided to send her a note inviting her to dinner. She agreed, and the outcome was a heady romance. They travelled to Berlin together shortly afterwards and witnessed the sad devastation of the city. He later followed her to Hollywood and lived with her while trying to obtain his naturalization papers. But he could never reconcile his love for her with the ambitions he had for his agency, which he was closer than ever to creating; and he had still not satisfied his desire to travel to the Soviet Union, which was something he had been wanting to do since the end of the war. He was to achieve this with John Steinbeck, whom he met when he returned to Paris from Hollywood in 1947. They had decided to collaborate on a book of photographs and text documenting the lives and hopes of ordinary Russians. While he awaited his visa, he set about making plans for the setting up of the photographers' cooperative. Somewhat sickened by the horrors of war which he had been witnessing for ten years, he decided that if he was going to remain a photographer it would have to be on his own terms. It was vital for him to be able to choose his assignments and the length of time they were to take, and to be clearly credited for his work. He greatly resented the way magazines such as *Life* retained the photographers' negatives, and he wanted greater control over how the stories were used and how they were resold. He had concluded that the only way to achieve this independence was by forming a union of photographers of such talent that their conditions could not be refused. The fact that he was also effectively out of a job once the war had come to an end provided additional motivation for setting up the agency. He persuaded Cartier-Bresson to collaborate with him on the project, and gained the backing of Len Spooner of the *Illustrated Magazine* in the form of a special agreement whereby Spooner would have first option on the photographs and proposals by the group of photographers. In return Spooner agreed to give the agency preferential terms, which included not only higher fees but also the payment of a large proportion of them in advance.

The final agreement for the founding of Magnum was signed in New York in May 1947 at the members' penthouse restaurant of the Museum of Modern Art. Present were Robert Capa, Cartier-Bresson, David (Chim) Seymour, as well as George Rodger, who had also been a correspondent for Time Inc., and William and Rita Vandivert. They agreed to contribute four hundred dollars each and that the agency would take forty per cent of the photographers' fees. And, typically of Capa, he also made everyone agree that members could borrow from the cash box in times of need. The name he chose for the agency spoke volumes for the ambitions he had for it. Not only was it inextricably linked to champagne and his personal sense of fun, it was also synonymous with glamour and, to those familiar with Latin, greatness. The fact that there was a famous gun of the same name certainly didn't go unnoticed either, and helped give the agency an aura of power in a world where photography was seeking to find a firm and permanent footing.

Magnum's innovations were primarily of a commercial and organizational nature, but the idea behind the cooperative could not have emanated from a purer or more honest sense of photography's need to be watched over and guided. What was in 1947 a tremendous step forward for photographers is common practice today. Instead of being at the mercy of the magazine editors, they would be able to control the use of their own time and assignments. Believing that much of post-war political history would depend on events in the developing countries, photographers wanted to be at greater liberty to travel in their chosen territories, spending as much time as was necessary to obtain the candid unobstrusive pictures they wanted, and receiving further assignments while they were there. Cartier-Bresson spent his time in India, George Rodger in Africa, and Chim in Europe.

Although Magnum was registered in New York, it was in Paris that it chose to make its base; and while the photographers' various destinations read like the index of an atlas, it was always to Paris that they returned. The first offices, which seemed more like a large apartment, were at 125 Rue du Faubourg St Honoré. Equipped with a long table for the purposes of editing, a telephone with a lengthy extension cord, and a sofa which acted as the agency's guest wing, it was home for an extraordinary cross-section of highly talented individuals of many nationalities. But they all had one thing in common: their love of photography. They would spend a great deal of time between assignments at the café downstairs discussing photography and hatching jobs, Capa conducting the conversation from his usual position at the pinball machine. Magnum soon became the focus of photographic interest in Europe and drew people from far and wide such as Ernst Haas and Inge Morath from Germany and Werner Bischof from Switzerland. Marc Riboud, Gisèle Freund and Herbert List were also early collaborators.

Lee Miller, too, through her friendship with Capa during the Liberation, became a member of Magnum. She had continued to cover the revival of the French *haute couture* for *Vogue*, but between stays at the Hôtel Scribe she also began to cover many of the war-related stories and accompanied the American army on its incursions beyond the Rhine. Her attention became more and more focused on the destruction and destitution left behind by the war, and it was largely due to her photographs at this time that the full genocidal horror of the concentration camps became known to the world. Miller, Capa and Eugene Smith were the first to visit Dachau. She was also

at Buchenwald, with George Rodger, William Vandivert and Margaret Bourke-White, who were covering the story for *Life*, before the last Germans had left the camp. In August 1945, after witnessing the carnage of Dachau, she spent a night at 27 Prinzenregenplatz in Munich, which turned out to have been Hitler's last residence. It was here that Dave Scherman took the memorable photograph of Lee in the Führer's bath. Her photographs, like so many taken by the early photojournalists, testified to the immense courage and determination they had to draw on to reveal to the world what had for so long been kept from its eyes.

Place de l'Hôtel de Ville
Capa 1944

Even though Paris had momentarily taken second place to the war as the object of the camera's attention, it remained throughout the nerve centre for all the changes which were taking place. As a style, photo-journalism had enormous consequences for the development of photography. The stories which Capa originated within Magnum and had the agency's photographers cover were an enormous success, notably the famous series 'How people are the world over', which ran for as long as eight months. Edward Steichen was to use the series as the source of inspiration for his 'Family of Man' exhibition at the Museum of Modern Art in New York in 1955. The show was seen by more people than any previous photographic exhibition. The style that had originated in the streets of Paris with Atget and Kertész had matured to become the banner of photography and, with Steichen's exhibition, was given its official seal of approval by New York.

On 25 May 1954, Robert Capa was killed by a landmine in Vietnam. A few days later news arrived that Werner Bischof had been killed in a car accident in the Peruvian Andes on 16 May. Chim took over the presidency of Magnum, but two years later in the summer of 1956 he, too, was killed during the Suez crisis. It was clearly the end of an era. Their style and courage would be perpetuated through Magnum, but without its guiding spirits the presence of the agency was greatly diminished. Despite the enormous impact which photo-journalism had on photography, and the strong presence it had in Paris, there was a quieter, less emphatic but equally evocative style developing which was intimately linked to the city.

In a small gallery in Paris in 1951 there was a group show called 'Paris Vu par le Groupe des XV'. This group had in fact been in existence since 1936 under the name of 'Le Rectangle', and under its new name since 1946. Its catalyst was Emmanuel Sougez, who ran the photo department at *L'Illustration* magazine and who had exhibited alongside Brassaï and Kertész in Julien Levy's European exhibition. His initial desire was to create an alternative context to that of Surrealism, Bauhaus and photo-journalism, in the same tradition as the Société Française de Photographie, which had not really moved forward with the times. The war never allowed the group to prosper, and even after it was re-founded photographic talk tended to revolve around Magnum. And yet the city's population of photographers was growing rapidly in the areas of the press, fashion and advertising, and the creation of the Groupe des XV marked an important point in the flowering of photographic activity that followed in the wake of Magnum's growing importance. Their work represented an accurate cross-section of post-war photography in Paris; it was to leave a poignant impression of the city after the Occupation and served as a role model for the many photographers who were less prepared to spend their time travelling around the world in search of subject-matter. Whereas Magnum functioned on an international level, the Groupe des XV had more modest and local aspirations. The fifteen members were elected annually by ballot and the single annual exhibition was always chosen by the group as a whole. Of the first exhibition it was said that there was a 'return to the classicism of Kertész, as powerfully expressive as it was seductive'.

The exhibition of 1951 on Paris featured several newcomers such as Robert Doisneau, Willy Ronis and René-Jacques, who all lived and worked in the city. The images which so captured the spirit of post-war Paris were taken for the most part in their free time, since they were obliged to rely on magazine stories and commercial work for their livelihood. But above all their importance lay in the refocusing of photography's gaze on to the city of Paris.

At one time a member of the Groupe des XV, Edouard Boubat bridged the gap between the photo-journalists and the more humanist school of photographers that was emerging. Boubat probably covered more distance across the globe than any photographer of his time, but he used Paris as a base from which to explore the world around him. From 1951, when he met Robert Frank and Eugene Smith, to the 1970s, he travelled extensively for the magazine *Réalités*. But one looks in vain in Boubat's work for the images of war, famine or earthquakes; his photographs are surrounded by a halo of peace and harmony. While photo-journalism was happy to play on our emotions with scenes of human tragedy, Boubat's reportage dealt with places where nothing seemed to happen, where goodness and a certain grace and serenity pervaded. In 1951 he was asked to do a reportage on 'The Artisans of Paris', and in the same year he exhibited in St Germain with Brassaï, Doisneau and Izis. Between trips he never tired of photographing Paris, conveying an unexpected beauty and an almost dreamlike quality in every street corner. Like the others in the group, Boubat had spent his childhood in a Paris of cobbled streets, courtyards and cellars, playing on those interminable stone steps with central handrails. Whereas in photo-journalism our attention is immediately drawn to the impact of the action, with Boubat there is always more than first meets the eye.

The magazines *Regards*, *Réalités* and *Paris Match* continued to publish the great photo-journalistic stories of the time, but through the new names associated with them, such as Jean-Philippe Charbonnier, Willy Ronis, Izis, Robert Doisneau and Boubat, there was a shift of emphasis towards a more humanist approach to witnessing world events. The disruption of the war had generated a real need to return to a

reconciliation of man and his environment. The world had seen enough images of devastation and was ready for a more tender vision. All the magazines eventually chose to print more light-hearted stories touching on tourism and lifestyle. The photographs which adorned their pages were used more as illustrations – informative, but full of human interest. While the photo-journalists were active in the far corners of the globe, these photographers contented themselves with what was on their doorstep, and Paris still presented an extraordinary background for the narrative pictures of its fun-fairs, parks and lovers. In 1945 the agency Rapho had regrouped

Hôtel Claridge,
Champs Elysées
Ronis 1948

many of the photographers, finding a new market in the publication of books, and in particular of books on Paris. In all, between 1949 and 1957, as many as ten compilations on the city were published by Doisneau, Izis and Willy Ronis alone.

Israël Bidermanas, or Izis, a Lithuanian Jew, was typical of the type of photographer who found himself representative of a style simply by virtue of his being in Paris. For Izis, as for many in the Groupe des XV, photography was a passion but not a livelihood. From being a printer he moved on to taking wedding photographs in order to make a better living for himself. It was only as the war was ending that, while hiding as a radio operator in the Limousin region of France, he began to take portraits of the soldiers. On returning to Paris he met Brassaï and Paul Eluard, who encouraged him greatly to continue with his work and assisted him in bringing out his first book, *Paris des Rêves* (*Paris of Dreams*), which was infused with a romanticism and tenderness far removed from the aggressive coverage of the war.

Like Izis, Robert Doisneau also began his career as an engraver before moving on to work for the sculptor Vigneau. To begin with, between 1934 and 1939, he was employed by Renault to take industrial photographs, and then, in 1948, by *Vogue* as a society photographer. It was only in the moments away from these commercial worlds that Doisneau discovered a whole universe for his photography in the people and the streets of Paris. While Doisneau's desire for human contact made him delight in his fellow man, Izis was attracted to the circuses and amusement parks for the sound of laughter and the sense of happiness they conveyed. Both allowed chance to determine their encounters, and if it has been said of their work that it makes the blind see, it is because of their ability to open our eyes to what is beautiful in the most mundane situations of our everyday lives.

Where Doisneau's sensitivity was with people, in the case of René-Jacques his poetry was often to be found in the street itself, still wet from the rain and empty of people, and with a melancholy made more poignant by the absence of human figures.

Willy Ronis was one of the many photographers of the period whose work

Autumn wind, Rue Royale
Doisneau 1952

became known through the pages of *Regards* magazine. From the very beginning of his career Ronis was attracted to assignments of a social nature, such as the reportage on the Rothschild Hospital and the return of the prisoners, which he was commissioned to do for the state railways. Ideologically and politically motivated, Ronis worked close to the working classes, covering strikes and union gatherings for the Communist Party as well as photographing the flea markets and poorer areas of the *banlieues*, the suburbs of Paris. But Ronis's style echoed that of Izis and Doisneau when he began to photograph two neighbouring quarters in Paris: Ménilmontant and Belleville. Until the late nineteenth century both were still villages perched on the top of two hills a short distance from the city and prided themselves on the vines and fruit trees which were grown on their slopes. The two villages, being the *quartiers pauvres* of Paris, have always provided the city with its labour force, and the inhabitants gained a reputation for participating in every possible insurrection, even after Napoleon III attempted to quell the unrest by splitting the community into two separate *arrondissements* in 1860. As late as the 1950s the two areas remained quite rural in atmosphere, and Ronis, aware of the transformations taking place, managed to capture many of those telling moments in a period of change when one knows that a place's heyday is over but there is still time to enjoy its decline. He witnessed the huge growth in Arab and African population and documented the destruction of the area to accommodate new housing. Ronis continues to photograph the neighbourhood today with all the intimacy of a man watching a former mistress growing old. Final proof that he had placed his finger on the pulse of the city was provided when Steichen met him in 1952 to choose images for his 'Family of Man' exhibition.

In his *History of Photography* Ian Jeffrey states that 'The Europeans sought to persuade themselves that nothing had changed, that their traditions survived . . . they rediscovered a France of rural artisans and folklore . . . a Paris where the lovers, the poets and the tramps basked along the Seine in the content and joyful city.' For many of the photographers this was indeed the case, but as a result they captured the city's very heartbeat and poetry through fragments of daily life, and they lent a tender nobility to the street life of simple people. They took on the role of the wandering minstrel, poet of the city, enchanted by it and enchanting in their vision of it. The simplicity of that vision emanated from a desire to create a new and stable moral order in which man could regain his lost faith, or at least to which one could turn for a moment of well-being.

In 1956 the Salon de la Photographie reopened. This helped to set in motion a gradual restructuring of the various photographic disciplines, of which two of the most important were advertising and fashion. Contrary to popular belief, advertising was far from being a derivative of photography's mainstream and had been a driving force in its development ever since Bauhaus had revealed that photography was a powerful visual and commercial aid. Advertising continued to employ photography in innovative ways and provided work for many photographers. It was through its revitalized relationships with fashion, however, that photography in Paris blossomed in the late 1950s.

At the outbreak of the war, Paris had lost most of its leading fashion photographers when they emigrated to New York. Erwin Blumenfeld and Horst P. Horst found work with *Vogue*, and Hoyningen-Huene and Martin Munkacsi began to collaborate with *Harper's Bazaar*. Thanks to the genius of the two magazines' art directors, Alexander Liberman and Alexei Brodovitch, fashion photography gained a new respect and admiration which was to place it firmly in the limelight. Brodovitch had spent ten years in Paris as a stage set designer, working to designs by Picasso and Matisse for Diaghilev's Ballet Russe. He went on to work for the magazine *Arts et Métiers Graphiques*, designing the layout of the magazine at the time when Kertész was being commissioned to take the photographs. For several years the photographers who had left Paris were the principal interpreters of the fashion of the day, sometimes joined by Cartier-Bresson. By the time Brodovitch and Liberman began to use the work of Richard Avedon and Irving Penn respectively for their innovative work around 1944, the thrust in fashion photography could be said to emanate almost entirely from New York and was predominantly American in spirit. Penn and Avedon effectively presided over their field of photography for more than a decade; and it was not until another New Yorker was sent to Paris in 1955 with a contract from *Vogue* as a fashion photographer that the next great shift in the medium occurred.

William Klein had spent some time in Paris in 1948 studying painting, in particular with Fernand Leger, who had been influential in getting him 'out of the studio and into the street'. During the time he spent in New York before returning to Paris to work for *Vogue*, he had picked up the camera and originated a style which went against everything which had gone before in the post-war era. His book *New York* appeared in both Paris and London, having failed to find a publisher in New

York, in 1956. It could not have shocked people more with its reactionary layout and candid disharmony. When Klein went into the street to take his fashion photographs it was with a set of principles directly opposed to those of Henri Cartier-Bresson; his approach was to confront the natural disorder of the crowds and all the ethnic and social symbolism that went with it. His technique was blatantly confrontational, sometimes going as far as accosting someone in the street in order to capture his reaction. He would even say of the act of photography that it was 'a transient moment in which one could seize the subconscious as well as the conscious'.

Although Klein was never wholly enamoured of fashion photography and used it chiefly as a means to support himself, some of the reactionary style apparent in *New York* changed the parameters of fashion photography and opened new doors for a great many people. It was in reply to Richard Avedon's dominant coverage of the Paris

Notre Dame
Boubat 1951

fashion collections for *Harper's Bazaar* that Alexander Liberman hired Klein in 1958 in an attempt to steal back the limelight for *Vogue*. Klein collaborated with *Vogue* for ten years but always maintained a certain distance, without which there would have been none of the defiant, inventive and sometimes venomous images that are among the most exciting photographs ever taken in fashion. He introduced wide-angle shots, multiple exposures and open flashes. People who inadvertently entered the frame of the picture were left in or cropped at the waist. The images were forcefully dynamic and on the very borders of what was accepted photographically. He placed his models among the dummies of the Musée Grévin, and painted out the faces of a crowd of onlookers in front of the Opéra. Curiously, his unorthodox and openly dramatic style only enhanced the glamorous niche that fashion was shaping for itself, and helped to launch it into the 1960s.

The Neo-Realist cinema of De Sica and Rosselini in Italy, as well as the realism which had filtered through from photo-journalism, gave added momentum to the transformation through which fashion photography had been going. Klein had used realism to great effect in his dramatic situations set up in the streets of Paris, and it was to influence another Paris-based photographer whom Klein introduced to *Jardin des Modes*, then one of the most *avant-garde* fashion magazines on the market.

When Frank Horvat settled in Paris in 1956, he was already well known as a photo-journalist through his collaborations with such magazines as *Life*, *Picture Post* and *Paris Match*. He brought with him from his photo-journalism not only his Leica, which enabled him to work closely and rapidly with his models, but also his incisive realism, as much in the setting of the models in various lifelike situations in the street as in their appearance. It is a great credit to Horvat's versatility that he joined Magnum in 1959 for a short while, working mainly for *Réalités*. Horvat had come to Paris early in his career to meet Henri Cartier-Bresson, who had advised him against mixing photo-journalism with fashion. Now, however, preferring the freedom which his fashion work accorded him, he chose to ignore the advice and returned to his fashion work, taking his Leica and his models into the streets of Paris.

Fashion itself was changing dramatically, especially in Paris, largely in response to an exuberant youth culture; *haute couture* was taking second place to *prêt à porter*, and with the strong support of *Elle* magazine, Klein and Horvat's work set the trend for a realist, anti-sophisticated style of fashion photography which they continued to produce for *Vogue* and *Harper's Bazaar* well into the 1960s. In many ways they had loosened up the medium and demonstrated photography's ability to fuse styles and marry apparent contradictions. They had also opened the way to young talent such as Jeanloup Sieff, Guy Bourdin and David Bailey, who all brought their own innovative styles to fashion photography.

At the beginning of the 1960s a number of disparate but important new elements combined to change Paris's relationship with photography for ever. In 1961 an Urban Commission was established to oversee the development of the city to accommodate the huge rise in population that had occurred in the last decade. Although the initial plans for the restructuring and renovation of Paris entailed the demolition of nearly a third of its residential quarters, the destruction was not to be as systematic as it had been under the Second Empire. It did, however, change the familiar skyline as the Tour Montparnasse was built and the business area of La Défense began to take shape. In the same year renovation work began on the buildings of architectural interest in quarters such as the Marais, in the course of which some of the last vestiges of the city's original charm were lost. The city's great appeal to foreigners began to be taken seriously and soon became more like a commercial enterprise as its heritage was institutionalized and promoted. The period of intense urban development also coincided with what has been termed 'the acceleration of history'; which in photography created a proliferation of styles and a multiplicity of directions.

A further assault on our collective memory of the city occurred in May 1968. The student riots of 11 May in the Latin Quarter saw thirty thousand demonstrators confront the forces of order to overturn, during the course of one night, a peaceful political regime which had been in power for ten years. Something of the poetic quietude which Paris had grown to embody, so powerfully conveyed by many photographers, disappeared overnight, and new political and social tensions grew which brought the city squarely into a new era. As a result the past became imbued with an aura of nostalgia which now so determines our vision of the city. The photographs which have recorded the city's evolution testify not only to its extraordinary beauty but also to photography's ability to weave past and present together in such a way that Paris's rich sociological and architectural history is ever-present. The power of the camera, when combined with the potent mixture of human perception and the passage of time, is such that the myth of Paris and its past has become a living legend.

Propaganda on the Champs Elysées
Schall 1943

Hôtel Meurice, Rue de Rivoli
Schall 1941

Shadow of the Bastille
Doisneau 1949

Shadow of the Institut de France
Ronis 1956

Boulevard Richard-Lenoir
Ronis 1946

Pont Neuf
Boubat 1948

'Scandale'
Bing 1947

Accordion player
Van Der Elsken 1950

Pont des Arts
Boubat 1948

A sideways glance
Doisneau 1948

Steps in the Rue Vilin, Belleville
Ronis 1959

Latin quarter
Boubat 1968

Ile de la Cité
Cartier-Bresson 1950

Palais Royal
Cartier-Bresson 1960

'Au chien qui fume' for 'Jardin des Modes'
Horvat 1957

The Opéra
Klein 1958

Strict intimacy, Montrouge
Doisneau 1945

The last waltz
Doisneau 1949

EUGENE ATGET
1856–1927

Atget was born in Libourne, France, but spent his early years in the suburbs of Paris with his artisan parents. When they died in 1861, he went to live with his uncle in Bordeaux. From 1875 he worked first as a cabin boy and then as a sailor on ships travelling to Africa from Marseilles, but returned in 1879 to study drama. He was a repertory actor for five years, working in Bordeaux and Paris, but left to take up painting and drawing. It was not until 1899 that he became interested in photography and bought a bellows camera. He began to produce photographic 'sketches' for artists (Man Ray, Derain and Utrillo) and also embarked on an extensive documentation of Paris.

Over a period of twenty-five years he photographed Parisian streets, buildings, tradespeople and shop fronts, selling over 2600 negatives to the Musée des Beaux Arts and numerous prints to the Bibliothèque Nationale. In 1926, the year his wife died, he met Berenice Abbott, who became his assistant and was instrumental in making his work known. Yet he died in poverty, having failed to make a successful living from his art.

EDOUARD DENIS BALDUS
1813–1882

Born in Westphalia, Germany, Baldus was painting portraits and religious scenes when he became interested in photography in 1849. Within two years his work was so highly regarded that he became a founder member of the Société Héliographique and received his first assignment from the Commission des Monuments Historiques to document the architectural monuments of France. Over the next thirty years he produced an important body of work in the best documentary tradition.

In 1852, he photographed the monuments of Paris and also published a guide to his new gelatin printing process. He then photographed landscapes in Dauphine and Auvergne, but returned to Paris to document the sculptures and architectural details of the new wing of the Louvre. In 1855 he was commissioned by de Rothschild to record the construction of the railroad from Paris to Boulogne and the resulting prints, together with his Auvergne landscapes, were exhibited at the World Fair of 1855 and won him a first-class medal.

In 1856, the year he became a French national, he was commissioned by the Ministry of the Interior to cover the flooding of the Rhône; in 1858 he photographed the official opening of the military harbour at Cherbourg, and in 1859 he was commissioned by de Rothschild to document the new stretch of railway from Paris to the Mediterranean. He finally returned to Paris in 1860 to complete his work on the monuments of the city.

HIPPOLYTE BAYARD
1801–1887

Born in Breteuil-sur-Noye, France, Bayard worked as a notary clerk before moving to Paris to become a civil servant in the Ministry of Finance. In 1837 he took up drawing and attended gatherings organized by Duval, meeting contemporary artists and learning about the advances in photography.

In 1839, the year that Daguerre's invention was publicly announced, Bayard also obtained a photographic image, but used a sensitized sheet of paper, not metal plate. His photographic drawings, or *photogénés*, were exhibited at an auction for the benefit of victims of a Martinique earthquake, and he submitted a report on his technique to the Académie des Sciences. He subsequently received a grant of 600 francs from the Ministry of the Interior, but little of the glory enjoyed by Daguerre, despite the importance and anteriority of his invention.

From 1842 onwards he photographed many views of Paris, in particular the windmills of Montmartre. In 1851 he was sent by the Commission des Monuments Historiques to Normandy, where he covered five regions. In the same year he invented a process to produce positives on paper with a one-second exposure time; he also co-founded the Société Héliographique Française.

In 1858 he opened a studio at 14 Port Mahon, moving in 1863, the year he was decorated Chevalier de la Légion d'Honneur, to 15 bis Boulevard de la Madeleine, where he formed a partnership with Bertall. Retiring in 1867, he went to live in Nemours, where he remained until his death.

AUGUSTE ADOLPHE BERTSCH
18??–1871

Little is known about the earlier part of Bertsch's life, but it is reported that, from 1851, he was active in scientific research, taking photographs of the antennae of flies, as well as lice and crystals. He played an important role in photography, improving the sensitivity of the collodion print in 1851 and introducing the disc-form shutter in 1852. He also co-founded the Société Française de Photographie in 1854.

In 1855 he invented an aparatus to enlarge prints and also sold prints of images seen through a microscope. Two years later he set up a portrait studio at 27 Rue Fontaine-Saint-Georges, Paris. His work was exhibited at the World Fairs of 1855 and 1857 and in 1858 he was named Chevalier de la Légion d'Honneur for his photographic work in the fields of science.

In 1860 he patented his miniature metal camera, the *chambre automatique*. This produced 20mm circular pictures, examples of which were shown the following year, enlarged with another of his inventions, the heliographic megascope. He retired in 1863, and because of hardship endured during the Seige of Paris, died eight years later.

ILSE BING
1899–

Ilse Bing was born in Frankfurt in 1899 and studied at the Universities of Frankfurt and Vienna. Having taught herself photography, she bought a Leica in 1929 and began taking photographs of *avant-garde* architecture and artists, as well as covering various stories for *Das Illustrierte Blatt*. In 1930 she emigrated to Paris, where she continued her portrait and documentary work but began to use the blurred, out-of-focus effect with which she became particularly associated.

In 1931 she met Julien Levy and was included in a New York exhibition of the work of European photographers. She photographed the Ballet Balanchine, and worked for *Harper's Bazaar* and Schiaparelli for several years. In 1936 H.W. van Loon, the critic and collector, invited her to New York. She arrived in 1941, having been interned at Camp de Gurs in 1940 while waiting for her visa. It was in New York that she was to meet and marry Konrad Wolff, a concert pianist.

Arriving with little more than her camera, she took portraits of children in their homes. From 1951 she became more interested in photographing objects and by 1957 had abandoned black and white for colour, doing all her own developing and printing. She stopped taking photographs a few years later and devoted herself to poetry, painting and collages, publishing *Words as Visions* in 1974 and *Numbers in Images* in 1976.

EDOUARD BOUBAT
1923–

Although born in Paris, Boubat spent much of his childhood with his grandmother in the Berry region of France. He worked in a photogravure workshop and sold his dictionaries to buy his first camera, a Rolleicord. In 1946 his first photograph, 'The Little Girl with the Autumn Leaves', was published and the following year he won the first prize at the Second Salon National de la Photographie.

In 1948 he started photographing daily life in the streets and cafés of Paris and in 1950 his work was published in *Camera*, with a text by Louis Stettner. The following year he exhibited at the Librairie La Hune alongside Brassaï, Doisneau and Izis and met Bertie Gilou of *Réalités* magazine, with whom he began a long collaboration. His first assignment was to photograph the artisans of Paris after which, in 1952, he travelled to Spain to cover the pilgrimage to Santiago de Compostela. He went on to spend four months in America before returning to France to become a permanent member of the team at *Réalités*.

Boubat worked with *Réalités* until 1967, when he became a freelance photographer. He has continued to travel throughout the world, photographing diverse subjects with a serenity of vision that has become his hallmark. He was awarded the Grand Prix du Livre at the Rencontres d'Arles in 1977.

BRASSAI
1899–1984

Born Gyula Halasz in Brasso, Transylvanian Hungary, it was not until 1925 that he adopted the name Brassaï. Educated in Hungary and Germany, he arrived in Paris as a journalist in 1924, was introduced to photography by Kertész in 1926 and started freelancing for the magazines *Minotaure* and *Harper's Bazaar*. He photographed the cafés, artists and streets of Paris and exhibited his first one-man show in 1931, the year his first book, *Paris de Nuit*, was published.

In 1934, he received the Emmerson medal in London and in 1937 the gold medal at the Daguerre Centenary Exhibition in Budapest. From 1936 to 1963, he collaborated with the magazines *Picture Post* and *Réalités*, after which he went on to photograph the work of Picasso in his studio, using some of the prints to illustrate his book *Conversations with Picasso*, published in 1964. He also designed stage sets for ballets and created the first workshop for photographic decor.

Brassaï was not only talented as a photographer and set designer, his sculptures and tapestries were widely exhibited and his film *Tant qu'il y aura des bêtes*, made in 1955, won a prize at Cannes. It was his photography, however, which was outstanding and was to win him numerous medals and awards – gold medal at the Venice Biennale in 1957; Photokina Obelisk in Cologne in 1963; the prize of the American Society of Magazine Photographers, with Ansel Adams, in 1966; the medal of the Town of Arles in 1974. The same year he was made Chevalier des Arts et des Lettres, and subsequently Chevalier de la Légion d'Honneur. In 1978 he was awarded the Premier Grand Prix National de la Photographie. By the time of his death, he had exhibited his photographs virtually throughout the world.

ROBERT CAPA
1913–1954

Robert Capa was born André Friedmann in Budapest. He studied political science at the University of Berlin and was an assistant photographer at Delaphots Agency before moving to Paris in 1933, where he changed his name and became a freelance photographer.

While working with *Life* and *Time* magazines, he helped create the Alliance Photo agency and started working for *Vu*. He photographed the Spanish Civil War in 1936 and subsequently published his first book, *Death in the Making*, in 1937. He photographed the Japanese invasion of China before emigrating to America, where he teamed up with *Life* magazine, returning to Europe at the outbreak of the Second World War.

In 1947 he travelled to Russia with John Steinbeck and was awarded the United States Medal of Freedom. The same year, with H. Cartier-Bresson, D. Seymour and G. Rodger, he founded Magnum Photos, of which he was President from 1952 to 1954. He spent two years in Israel and rejoined *Life* magazine, as a naturalized American citizen, to cover what was to be his sixth and last war for them.

Capa died in Thai Bình, Indo-China on 25 May 1954 when he stepped on a mine. He was posthumously awarded the French Croix de Guerre avec Palmes, the George Polk Memorial Award, and the Gold Medal of the Overseas Press Club of America. His autobiography, *Slightly out of Focus: Images of War*, was published in 1964.

HENRI CARTIER-BRESSON
1908–

Cartier-Bresson was born in Cantaloupe, France and educated in Paris. He studied painting with Cottonet and Jacques Emile Blanche before joining the studio of André Lohte in 1927. From 1928 he was a student of painting and literature at Cambridge University, until he returned to France for military service in 1930.

In 1931 he began to take photographs and three years later was taken on as photographer for an ethnographic expedition to Mexico. In 1935, he became a freelance photographer in New York whilst studying cinematographic technique with Paul Strand, and was appointed assistant to Jean Renoir in 1936. He made a documentary with William Klein entitled *Retour à la Vie* in 1937 and a year later photographed the Coronation of George VI.

A corporal in the photographic section of the army during the Second World War, he was imprisoned in the Vosges and Germany, but managed to escape on both occasions and was present to photograph the Liberation of Paris. After the war he made a film entitled *Le Retour* and later returned to being a freelance photographer. In 1947 he was asked by Capa to be a co-founder of Magnum Photos and a year later set off to photograph many of the Eastern Countries (India, Burma, Pakistan, China and Indonesia). In 1954 he travelled to the Soviet Union, having already received two of his four Overseas Press Club Awards and subsequently continued to travel extensively throughout China, Cuba, Mexico and Canada.

He left Magnum Photos in 1966, although his work continued to be represented by the agency. In 1970 he married Martine Franck, now also a member of Magnum Photos, and although he continues to take photographs, he has devoted himself to drawing, becoming a member of the American Academy of Arts and Sciences in 1974.

LOUIS-JACQUES MANDE DAGUERRE
1787–1851

Born in Cormeilles-en-Parisis, Daguerre studied design in an architect's office in Orléans for two years before moving to Paris to work as a scenery painter and stage decorator at the Paris Opera House. From 1807 to 1815 he assisted Prévost in painting panoramas and by 1822 his own dioramas were shown in Paris, appearing in London the following year.

In 1823 Giroux, a relation of his wife, Louise Georgina Arrowsmith, started selling his *dessins-fumées* and in 1826 Daguerre offered one to Niepce, who was working on the photographic process. In return, Daguerre received 'La Sainte Famille', the result of Niepce's early experiments. Eventually the two men met, forming a photographic partnership in 1829. Although Niepce died in 1833, Daguerre went on to photograph various scenes of Paris – the first photographs of the city.

In 1839, his success in fixing an image on a silvered plate was announced to the Académie des Sciences by Count François Arago. Daguerre was made an Officier de la Légion d'Honneur by King Louis-Philippe, and was awarded the Order of Merit by the King of Prussia for his invention. By the end of 1839, both his apparatus and technical guides were being sold at Giroux and Susse Frères. He retired to Bry-sur-Marne in 1841 and although he took up painting, he continued to experiment with photography, inventing a process for albumen prints in 1843.

ROBERT LEON DEMACHY
1859–1936

Demachy was born at Saint Germain-en-Laye, the son of the founder of the Demachy Bank. Although he joined the family business, he was passionate about music, painting, photography and cars. He volunteered for the French Navy in 1877 but turned to photography full-time in 1888, having become a member of the Société Française de Photographie in 1882 and won two medals for his photographs the following year.

In 1894, as a founder member of the Photo Club de Paris, he served on the editorial committee of *La Revue de Photographie*, and exhibited his portraits and landscapes. In 1896, having greatly popularized the gum-bichromate technique, he wrote articles on the legitimacy of the manipulations employed by the new school of photography, which he was to champion. In 1897 he exhibited with Puyo, turning to Pictorialism in 1902.

In 1903 he contributed to *Camera Work* and Stieglitz's exhibitions in New York. He became an honorary member of the Royal Photographic Society in 1905 and joined the Linked Ring movement. From 1906 he made oil prints with Puyo and published *Art Processes in Photography* at the Photo Club de Paris. He continued to use the oil transfer process until he abandoned photography for

drawing in 1914. In the year of his death, he donated all his exhibited works to the Société Française de Photographie.

ROBERT DOISNEAU
1912–

Born in Gentilly on the outskirts of Paris, Doisneau studied engraving and lithography before becoming a lettering artist to a pharmaceutical company, where he learned about photography. He assisted André Vigneau in 1931 and the following year had his first photographs published in *Excelsior*. From 1934 he was an industrial photographer for the Renault factory in Boulogne, but was fired in 1939 for lack of punctuality and went to join the Light Infantry.

In 1942 he met Maximillien Vox and illustrated his first scientific book. He spent 1945 with the Alliance Photo agency but joined Rapho in 1946 and, with Blaise Cendrars, started a book on the suburbs of Paris. He won the Prix Kodak in 1947 and the following year joined *Vogue*, although his time as a society photographer was brief and he preferred to work on his book projects. In 1956 he was awarded the Prix Niepce.

In 1968 he reported on the effects of fifty years of Communist rule in the USSR for *La Vie Ouvrière*. A film entitled *Le Paris de Robert Doisneau* was made with F. Porcile in 1973 and in 1975 he was invited to exhibit at the Rencontres d'Arles. Several documentary films have since been made about Doisneau's work and his vision of Paris – he still lives and works in the suburbs of the city.

LEON GIMPEL
1878–1947?

Born in 1878, Léon Gimpel bought his first camera when he was nineteen. In 1899 he started experiments with night-time photography, using the ducks in the Bois de Boulogne as subjects. His first story was published in 1900 and was the result of a remarkable coincidence – he was given a press card by his nephew in order to attend a performance at the Théâtre Français, but the theatre caught fire and he was able to photograph the whole incident. In 1904 he started what was to be a thirty-year collaboration with *Illustration* magazine and in 1908 he joined the Société Française de Photographie. Two years later he documented the effects of the severe floods on both Paris and Versailles.

FRANK HORVAT
1928–

Born in Abbazia, Italy, Frank Horvat was educated in Milan and Lugano, Switzerland, where his parents emigrated during the Second World War. In 1944 he sold his stamp collection to buy his first camera, a Retina.

He studied at the Fine Arts Academy of Brera, Italy, and in 1950 joined an advertising agency as a graphic designer. The same year, his first colour photographs made the front cover of the magazine *Epoca* and he took up photography professionally. His first freelance reportage, 'Pilgrimage in Northern Italy' was in 1951, the year he travelled to Paris to meet Capa and Cartier-Bresson, and started working for *Paris Match*.

From 1952 to 1954 he travelled to India, publishing work in *Paris Match*, *Picture Post* and *Life*. He based himself in London for a year before returning to Paris in 1955, where he joined the Rapho agency and started working with the magazine *Réalités*. In 1957 *Camera* dedicated an issue to his series 'Paris au téléobjectif'.

From 1957 onwards, Horvat moved more towards fashion photography in an innovative way which successfully harnessed a documentary style to the needs of the fashion magazines. After a brief affiliation with Magnum, he was commissioned in 1962 by the German journal *Revue* to photograph all the great capitals of the world. In 1976 he began a series of photographs on the trees of the world, which culminated in a book.

From 1980 to 1983 he worked on a series of portraits of women in the style of famous paintings. Today, Frank Horvat lives and works in Paris and has become a leading expert on the use of computer technology in photography.

IZIS
1911–1980

Izis was born Israël Bidermanas in Mariampolé, Lithuania. From 1924 he apprenticed as a photographer until, in 1927, he set off with a friend to explore and photograph his homeland. In 1930 he moved to Paris and a year later took over the management of a photography shop in the Rue Nationale. When the war broke out, he left Paris for the Limosin region, where he earned a living retouching local photographers' prints. In 1944 he was taken prisoner by the Germans and, on his release, moved toward documentary photography.

In 1947, a French citizen by marriage, he returned to Paris and set up a studio. He began freelancing for the new magazine *Paris Match* and met Chagall, who encouraged him in his work. In 1951 Izis went to London with Jacques Prévert for the book *Les Charmes de Londres* and from 1952 to 1969 was under contract to *Paris Match*. From 1963 to 1964 he photographed Chagall's work on the ceiling of the Paris Opéra and in 1965 worked on a television programme, *Chambre Noir*, with the writer Michel Tournier. In 1978 Izis, alongside William Klein and Lisette Model, was guest of honour at the Rencontres d'Arles.

RENE-JACQUES
1908–

Born René Gitou in Phnom Penh, Cambodia, René-Jacques first started taking photographs in 1925. He won first prize in an amateur photography contest in Royan in 1927 and three years later gave up a literary career to become a photographer. His first pictures were published in *Plan* and he was subsequently in demand for his portraits and interiors, as well as industrial and cinema work.

He became a member of the Société Française de Photographie in 1936, the same year that he took part in an exhibition at the Royal Photographic Society in London. He was a film-set photographer until the outbreak of the Second World War, when he joined the army as a lieutenant.

He photographed many of the old hotels in Paris and produced a series of books for 'Paris à travers les Siècles'. He illustrated *Trésors Méconnu de Paris* and became a member of the Groupe des XV, with whom he went on to exhibit. In 1947 he opened a studio in Paris and the following year won first prize at the Salon National de la Photographie, the same year that he travelled to Germany to photograph the destruction left by the war.

In 1949 René-Jacques exhibited his cinema photographs at the Twenty-First Salon de la Photographie. He photographed the Renault factories in Boulogne-Billancourt, Flins et Leman, winning first prize for his colour landscapes at the Sixth Salon National de la Photographie. In 1954 he began collaborating with *Holiday* and *Harper's Bazaar* and exhibited in the Musée Réattu in Arles. In 1956 he participated in the exhibition 'L'Alphabet de Paris' alongside Cartier-Bresson, Ronis, Izis, Brassaï and many others. He was nominated President of

the National Association of Photographers in 1962. He lives in Paris and continues to photograph, although he abandoned commercial work in 1975 to work on his own projects.

ANDRE KERTESZ
1894–1985

Kertész was born in Budapest. At the age of six, he discovered instructions in an attic on how to take photographs and began to dream of becoming a photographer. When his father died in 1909 he was put into his uncle's care, becoming a student at the Academy of Commerce a year later, and joining the stock exchange in 1912. He bought his first camera in 1913 and started to work as a photographer, but was obliged to join the army the following year. He was wounded at Göttz and paralysed for a year, and when, in 1918, the majority of his negatives and plates were destroyed, he returned to work at the stock exchange.

He moved to Paris in 1925 and made a living selling his photographs for 25 francs a print. He began to work with many international newspapers and magazines and, in 1927, was offered his first one-man show in Paris. In 1928 he bought his first Leica and started reporting for the magazine *Vu*.

He married in 1933 and published his first book, *Enfants*. With war approaching he settled in New York, working for Keystone agency. He continued to live in New York until his death but started to work for fashion magazines, particularly for Condé Nast, with whom he was associated until 1962, when he left due to ill health to spend the rest of his life taking photographs for his own pleasure.

WILLIAM KLEIN
1928–

William Klein was born and educated in New York. He worked mainly as a painter and although he obtained his first camera in the late 1940s (he won it through a game of poker) he did not begin to take photographs until some years afterwards. He exhibited his paintings in Paris in 1948, where he had come to study painting, but returned to New York in 1954, keeping a photo-journal of the city which later became a book, *New York*. Published in Paris and London, it earned him the Nadar prize. From 1955 to 1965 he was under contract to American *Vogue* as a fashion photographer, although he also made

several films. In 1963 he was named one of the thirty most important photographers in history by Photokina, but soon after abandoned photography to concentrate on film-making. He won the Grand Prix International at Tours for his film *Cassius the Great* in 1965 and the Jean Vigo Prize in 1966 for his film *Who are you Polly Maggoo?*

It wasn't until 1978, several films later, that he took up photography again and was invited as the guest of honour at the Rencontres d'Arles. He has continued to make films for television and advertising both in America and France, as well as to take photographs in a style which became popular as a vibrant antithesis to photo-journalism and the 'Ecole de Paris' photography.

JACQUES-HENRI LARTIGUE
1894–1986

Born in Courbevoie, Lartigue moved with his family to Paris in 1899. He took his first photograph at the age of six and received his first camera two years later.

As a young boy photography became a passion and he began to keep a detailed photographic diary of his life. From the games he played as a child, he went on to photograph sports such as horse racing, tennis and automobile racing but remained an amateur photographer. In 1914 he enrolled as a volunteer in the army where, in spite of painting courses at the Académie Julien, he remained until 1918. He exhibited his paintings internationally in 1922 and continued to do so until 1978.

In 1932 he photographed and acted as assistant director on the film *Le Roi Dansole* and from 1935 illustrated many fashion magazines with his drawings. It was not until the 1950s that his photographs started to appear in the press. Lartigue was Vice-President of the association Gens d'Images in 1954 and exhibited in the group photography shows at the Galerie D'Orsay in 1955 and 1956.

His real recognition came in 1963 when the Museum of Modern Art in New York gave him his first one-man show and then, in 1965, he published his *L'Album de Famille*. The publication of *Diary of a Century* in 1970 showed his early work and was received as a refreshing antidote to his contemporaries, the Pictorialists. His first French retrospective was at the Musée des Arts Decoratifs in 1975 and again contributed to popularizing his humorous insight into a charming personal world.

HENRI LE SECQ
1818–1882

Born in Paris, Le Secq studied painting in the studios of Pradier and Granger, before joining Le Gray, Nègre and Fenton in 1840 to study with Paul Delaroche. He studied photography under Gustave Le Gray from 1848 to 1849, and was one of the first photographers to produce large calotype views of the cathedrals of Reims, Strasbourg, Amiens and Chartres, before their restoration by Viollet-le-Duc. From 1850 to 1853 he photographed the architectural monuments of Amiens and Paris, including many of the changes wrought by Haussmann. Some of his pictures were published in 1851 in Blanquart-Evrard's album *Paris Photographique*.

He was a founding member of the Société Héliographique in 1851 and was appointed by the Commission des Monuments Historiques to photograph the regions of Champagne, Alsace and Lorraine. Between 1855 and 1856 he produced numerous still lives and landscapes from his home in Normandy, but ultimately abandoned photography to devote himself to painting and drawing as well as expanding his collection of ironwork.

CHARLES MARVILLE
1816–1879?

Charles Marville was born in Paris. An artist, lithographer and illustrator, he first started taking photographs in 1851, printing on calotype, salted or albumenized paper. Between 1852 and 1853 he travelled, first to Algeria, then through central France, and finally to Germany, producing a series of negatives which were published in the Blanquart-Evrard album, *Art Réligieux*. From 1854 to 1860 Marville worked from a studio at 27 Rue Saint Dominique in Paris.

In 1858 he was commissioned by the government to photograph Old Paris and to document the many changes which were taking place in the city under Haussmann. Marville moved his studio in 1861 to 6 Rue de la Grande Chaumière, but left soon afterwards to photograph Old Master drawings in Milan and Turin. In 1862 he was appointed photographer to the Imperial Museum of the Louvre, the City of Paris and King Victor Emmanuel of Italy, receiving, in the same year, the Italian Gold Medal for photography. He photographed the Domaine de la Bagatelle extensively in 1867 and also the destruction and the ruins of the Commune in 1871.

WILLY MAYWALD
1907–1985

Born in Cleves, Germany, Willy Maywald attended the Fine Art School of Berlin and worked as an assistant to the director in a film studio before going to Paris in 1931. There he learned photography from Harry Meerson and opened his own studio in 1934, covering fashion and portraiture for the many French and international magazines. He had his first exhibition in Paris in 1935 with Dora Maar and Pierre Boucher.

From 1939 to 1940 he was detained in various internment camps in France, finally taking refuge in Switzerland in 1942. Throughout the Second World War, however, he took many portraits of artists, writers, architects and actors, moving on to become photographer to Christian Dior in 1947.

In 1949, he exhibited in Paris, New York and Hollywood, to introduce his book *Artists at Home*. He received the first prize at Photokina in Cologne in 1952 and the medal for best fashion photograph in Munich in 1959.

During the 1960s, Willy Maywald worked mainly for architectural magazines, although he continued to take portraits of the famous. In 1971 he set up exhibitions of his work, which were to tour internationally throughout the decade.

LEE MILLER
1907–1977

Born in Ploughkeepsie, New York, Lee Miller, after a period in Paris in 1925 studying theatre technique, became a model for Condé Nast and began to appear on the front covers of *Vogue*.

In 1929 she left modelling in New York to return to Paris, was introduced to Man Ray and became his assistant. In 1932 she exhibited twice at the Julien Levy gallery in New York, where she later returned to set up a photographic studio with her brother, Erik.

In 1934 Lee Miller married Aziz Eloui Bey and went to live in Egypt, but returned to Paris in 1938, this time with a photographic style which had become photo-journalistic. At the outbreak of the Second World War, she joined the staff of *Vogue* in London and photographed scenes of the Blitz, which were later published in *Grim Glory: Pictures of Britain under Fire*. She was accredited as US Forces War Correspondent and went on to publish *Wrens in Camera*. From 1944 she covered the war in Europe, writing articles as well as taking photographs.

After the war she remained on the continent, notably in Vienna and Bucharest, photographing the plight of children in hospitals. She continued to photograph for *Vogue* until 1949, when she moved to Sussex with her second husband, Roland Penrose. In 1954 she illustrated his book *Picasso: His Life and Work* and the following year exhibited in Steichen's 'Family of Man' Exhibition at the Museum of Modern Art in New York.

By 1960, Lee Miller had virtually abandoned photography, although she illustrated her husband's book on Anton Tapies and in 1976, the year before her death from cancer, she was invited to deputize for Man Ray at the Rencontres d'Arles.

CHARLES NEGRE
1820–1880

Born in Grasse, Provence, Charles Nègre was taught drawing by Pezetti in Aix-en-Provence until he moved to Paris in 1839, where he studied painting under Delaroche. In 1843 he left to study under Michel Drolling and later Ingres, and exhibited at every Salon des Beaux Arts in Paris between 1845 and 1853.

In 1847 he began to take photographs in earnest, registering a formula for making daguerreotypes with a shorter exposure, which he used to document his paintings. In 1851 he invented his own equipment for instantaneous exposures and moved to the South of France, the following year beginning his album of the Midi, which consists of approximately 200 negatives.

He started using Niepce's engraving process in 1854, and then gilding by electro plating; by 1856 he had patented a heliographic engraving process which was bought by the Russians for 8000 francs.

He was awarded a silver medal at the Amsterdam World Fair of 1855 and a first-class medal in Paris for his work, after which he started to receive commissions from the government. He left Paris in 1861 for Nice, returning briefly in 1862, when he brought out a book for Prince Léopold of Belgium. He opened a school in Nice, where he taught drawing, but continued to photograph until his death in Grasse.

COMMANDANT CONSTANT PUYO
1857–1933

Born in Morlaix, France, Constant Puyo attended La Fère Artillery School, becoming an artillery officer and later commandant. He started taking photographs in 1885 and, with

Demachy and Bucquet, co-founded the Photo Club de Paris in 1894. He co-exhibited with Demachy in 1897 and later retired from the army to devote himself entirely to photography and technical research.

Puyo wrote extensively about the gum-bichromate process, and with its use became a leading exponent of 'Pictorial' photography. From 1904 to 1906 he had a series of lenses made, including a telephoto lens of variable focus for photographing landscapes. He was awarded the Janssen Medal of the Société Française de Photographie in 1908, and at the International Congress of Photography in Brussels in 1910 gave a seminal paper on Pictorialism.

He became Chairman of the Photo Club de Paris in 1921 and a member of the Société Française de Photographie in 1924, but retired to Morlaix the same year, concentrating on portrait and landscape photography.

MARC RIBOUD
1923–

Marc Riboud was born in Lyon, France. His father gave him his first camera at the age of six, a pocket Kodak, which he used to photograph the châteaux of the Loire Valley. When his father died in 1939, he inherited his Leica.

During the war, Riboud was a member of the Resistance, after which he studied engineering in Lyon. In 1951, he took photographs at the festivals of Lyon and Avignon, which were published in *Art et Théâtre de France* and, after meeting Henri Cartier-Bresson, decided to pursue photography as a profession. His simple but powerful humanistic style enabled him to join Magnum Photos in 1952, the year in which he also produced the now famous series of photographs of the painter on the Eiffel Tower, which was published by *Life* magazine.

He moved to London in 1954, becoming a full-time member of Magnum Photos a year later, and began to travel extensively, visiting India, China, the United States, Africa, Vietnam, Israel, Czechoslovakia and Iraq. He won the Overseas Press Club Award for his books *The Three Banners of China* in 1966 and *The Faces of North Vietnam* in 1970.

He had moved back to Paris by 1968, however, in time to cover the student riots of May 1968 and De Gaulle's death in 1970. He became President of Magnum Photos from 1975 to 1976 but resigned as a full-time

member in 1980, although he remained a contributing photographer.

He was given retrospective exhibitions at the Musée d'Art Moderne in Paris in 1989 and at the International Center for Photography in New York in 1988, and continues to live and work in Paris.

WILLY RONIS
1910–

Born in Paris, the son of a photographer, Willy Ronis received his first camera at the age of sixteen and began taking photographs of the city, which he continues to do today. In 1932 he joined his father's studio in Boulevard Voltaire and by 1936, the year of his father's death, he had had his first publications in the press. He bought a Rolleiflex and became a freelance photographer, working for the Illustrated Press. He later moved more towards photography of a social documentary nature and travelled throughout Greece, Yugoslavia and Albania. During the Second World War, he held a variety of posts, from manager of a theatrical troup to cinema decorator's assistant, as well as a portrait photographer's assistant in the Unoccupied Zone, before returning to Paris in 1944.

After becoming a member of the Groupe des XV, he joined the Rapho agency. While working in both fashion and advertising he won the Prix du Salon National in 1954; he also covered industrial subjects. He started using a 35mm camera and went on to win the Kodak prize and to receive a gold medal at the Venice biennale in 1957.

During the 1960s he produced photographic illustrations for numerous stories on Algiers and Eastern Europe. In 1972 he left Paris for the South of France, teaching and lecturing in Avignon, Aix-en-Provence and Marseilles. He won the Grand Prix National des Arts et des Lettres (photo) in 1979 and undertook various projects for the Ministry of Culture. In 1980 he was the guest of honour at the Rencontres d'Arles and won, in 1981, the Prix Nadar for his book *Sur le Fil du Hazard*.

ROGER SCHALL
1904–

Roger Schall, the son of a photographer, was born in Nancy. He and his family moved to Paris in 1911, but left for Sables d'Onne in 1917, where he started his first job as a draughtsman. In 1920 he was taught

photography by his father and returned to Paris to work as an industrial and interior photographer.

He did his military service in Strasbourg in 1924, working as a painter, and the following year was posted to the Lebanon in the photographic section. In 1926 he returned to work with his father and in 1929 began to collaborate with *Paris* magazine alongside Brassaï, Kertész and Moral. In 1931 he opened his own studio in Montmartre and began working for *L'Art Vivant* and *Vu*.

After a brief spell working for *Vogue*, he was sent by *Vu* to Berlin to cover the Olympic Games and had work published in *Die Dame* and *Berliner Illustrierte*. In 1938 he worked for the first issue of *Paris Match* and travelled to Morocco with the writer Colette. He started working with *Life* magazine in 1939 and was commissioned to photograph the work camps in Switzerland.

When war broke out he was assigned to the Second Army based at Verdon, but soon returned to Paris to photograph the city life. In 1943, he travelled to Corsica to complete his book *Reflets de France*, which was finally published in 1960. In 1944 he produced photographs advertising couturiers' perfumes, while his brother, Raymond, published the book *A Paris sous la Botte des Nazis*.

In 1967 Roger Schall's son, Jean Frédéric, took over the photographic studio in Montmartre.

THE SEEBERGER FAMILY
JULES 1872–1932; LOUIS 1874–1946; HENRI 1876–1956; JEAN 1910–1979; ALBERT 1914–

Jules, Louis and Henri Seeberger were born in France of a Bavarian father, who became a naturalized Frenchman in 1886. They were educated in Lyon and then at the Lycée Rollin in Paris. Jules became interested in photography in 1892 and was the first to buy a camera. Although he photographed Montmartre in 1898, it was after winning first prize at the 'Lecture Pour Tous' contest some time later that he decided to become a photographer. Henri Seeberger, in the meantime, had set up a painting studio.

Both Henri and Jules submitted prints in the first photographic contest organized by the Ville de Paris in 1904, the same year that Leopold Verger commissioned them to photograph the major provincial cities. The results of many of these trips, which continued until 1909, were turned into postcards.

In 1907 all three brothers won gold medals from the Ville de Paris for their photographs of 'Les Jardins des Plantes', 'The Luxembourg Gardens', and 'Suburban Houses'. From 1909 they began to take fashion photographs, and were commissioned by the director of the magazine *Mode Pratique* to photograph models in outdoor scenes. In 1910 they photographed the floods of Paris and set up a studio at 33 Rue de Chabrol, from where they worked for *Le Monde et Science*, *Jardin des Modes*, *L'art et la Mode* and *Vu*.

Louis and Henri were both called up in 1914 and although they went back to photography after the war, their brother Jules drifted towards painting and gave up photography altogether in 1925.

Louis had two sons, Jean and Albert, who also became photographers. Between 1923 and 1931 they were commissioned by a Hollywood agency to document Paris to help with the construction of sets of the city for the cinema. In 1941 the two brothers re-opened the family studio, doing fashion and photo-journalistic work until the Occupation, which they were also able to photograph.

In 1946, Jean became a co-founder of the Groupe des XV. Two years later, the brothers moved to 112 Boulevard Malsherbes, abandoning portraiture in order to concentrate on fashion.

EDWARD STEICHEN
1879–1973

Born in Luxembourg, Steichen emigrated to Michigan in 1881. He apprenticed as a lithographer in Milwaukee, where he moved in 1894, before attending art school. He took his first photographs in 1896 and exhibited in the Second Salon of Philadelphia in 1899. The following year he moved to Paris to study painting at the Académie Julien and, while there, sent photographs to the Chicago Photo Salon, where they were noticed by Stieglitz.

In 1901 he exhibited photographs of Rodin and his sculptures in the Maison des Artistes in Paris. He joined the Linked Ring movement and on his return to New York co-founded the Photo-Secession movement with Stieglitz and had his photographs published in the second issue of *Camera Work*.

He went back to Paris in 1906 and organized exhibitions of the work of artists such as Matisse, Rodin, Brancusi and Picasso for Stieglitz's 291 Gallery in New York. In 1914 he returned to America and established an aerial photography department for the US Air Force.

In 1922 he gave up painting, opened his own studio in New York to photograph portraits and fashion, and became *Vogue*'s main photographer in 1923. During the Second World War, he organized the War Photography Department of the US Navy and, in 1947, became Director of Photography at the Museum of Modern Art in New York. Steichen organized over fifty exhibitions for the museum, the most important being 'The Family of Man' in 1955. He retired in 1962 and published his autobiography in 1963. He became Commander of the Order of Merit in 1966 and died seven years later in West Redding.

ALFRED STIEGLITZ
1864–1946

Born in Hoboken, New Jersey, Stieglitz was educated in America and Germany. In 1883 he took his first photographs while working with H.W. Vogel and went on to win a prize in a competition held by *Amateur Photographer* magazine in 1887.

In 1890 he returned to New York and became a partner in a photogravure firm. He went freelance in 1892, collaborating with a number of magazines as well as acting as Editor-in-Chief of American *Amateur Photographer*. He travelled to Europe in 1894, exhibiting in the first International Salon at the Photo Club de Paris, and became a member of the Linked Ring movement.

In 1896, when the Society of Amateur Photographers and the New York Camera Club merged, he became Vice-President of the new Camera Club of New York. A year later he launched *Camera Notes*, a journal of the Camera Club, publishing Pictorialist photogravures. In 1899 Stieglitz had his first one-man show and left *Camera Notes* to found the Photo-Secession movement, whose first exhibition concentrated on the Pictorialists.

In 1903 he became Publisher and Director of *Camera Work*, whose graphic section was controlled by his friend and advisor, Edward Steichen. He received the Progess Medal from the Royal Photographic Society in 1905 and went on to open The Little Gallery, also known as '291', a few years later. In 1917, he began taking pictures of Georgia O'Keeffe, whom he married seven years later. He was to open further galleries, including the Intimate Gallery in 1925 and the American Place Gallery in 1929. Despite his desire not to leave his work for posterity, the Metropolitan Museum was able to convince him to do otherwise.

DENNIS STOCK
1928–

Born and educated in New York, Dennis Stock trained as a photographer with Gjon Mili from 1947. In 1951 he became a freelance photographer and won first prize in the annual Young Photographers Contest, held by *Life*, for his photographs of East German refugees. His reputation as a photo-journalist with *Life* enabled him to join Magnum the same year.

In 1955 he met and photographed James Dean and published *Portrait of a Young Man – James Dean* a year later. From 1957 to 1970 he photographed the jazz world throughout America, holding his first one-man show in 1963.

During the 1970s he gave workshops and lectures in New York and travelled to Italy and Japan. In 1977 he was invited as an exhibitor and lecturer by the Rencontres d'Arles and when he was invited a second time, in 1979, he moved to Provence. He continues work as a photo-journalist and divides his time between the US and Provence.

WILLIAM HENRY FOX TALBOT
1800–1877

Born in Melbury, Dorset, Talbot was educated in England and attended Cambridge University, where he read mathematics and physics. He travelled to Italy with a Camera Lucida as a drawing aid in 1823 and on a subsequent trip in 1833 became interested in capturing the image projected by the Camera Obscura, with which he was then working.

After a brief spell in parliament (1833–4) for Chippenham, he retired and dedicated his time to his photographic experiments with sensitized paper. In 1835 he discovered the principle of the negative; in 1836 he was elected to the Council of the Royal Society, and with the invention of the daguerreotype in 1839, he became interested in the advances in photography taking place across the Channel.

In 1840 Talbot discovered that the sensitized paper exposed in the copying camera contained a 'latent image', which he patented, calling it the 'calotype'. He opened a studio for photographic reproductions in Reading in 1844 and published collections of his calotypes – *The Pencil of Nature*, followed by *Sun Pictures* in 1845. He retired from photography around 1860, taking up botany, research in electromagnetism and astrology.

Talbot was awarded a gold medal in

London in 1862 and became an honorary member of the Royal Photographic Society in 1873 for his enormous contribution in the fields of photography and science.

EDOUARD VAN DER ELSKEN
1925–1990

Born in Amsterdam Van der Elsken studied painting and drawing until the outbreak of the Second World War, when he joined the Resistance. In 1945 he became an apprentice in a photographic laboratory, and, in 1947, turned to photography full-time.

He arrived in Paris in 1950 with only a Leica and two rolls of film, living under the bridges and photographing in cafés by night. Later the same year he started working as a correspondent for a Dutch newspaper, while also documenting the life of a Canadian singer in Saint Germain des Près. In 1953 he returned to the Netherlands and set up a studio in Edam in 1955, the year he was given his first one-man show in Chicago. In 1956 he published *A Love Story in Saint Germain des Près*, for which he received international acclaim. He also travelled to the Central African Republic, where he spent several months living with and photographing a local tribe.

Backed by a shipping company and a Dutch TV network, Van der Elsken toured the world for fourteen months during 1961 and 1962 – the result of which was a book entitled *Sweet Life*. In 1971 he was awarded the Netherlands National Film award. In 1980 he published a book on Amsterdam and its photographers and the following year another book on Paris and its photographers. During the late 1980s he spent much time in Japan.

PHOTOGRAPHIC ACKNOWLEDGEMENTS

The publishers wish to thank the following copyright holders for permission to reproduce the photographs contained in this book, which are identified by page number: Agence Top/E. Boubat, half-title, 94, 114, 121, 124, 127; Anneke van der Elsken, 123; Arch. Phot. Paris/DACS ., 29, 66; Association des Amis de Jacques-Henri Lartigue, 38, 43, 59, 60, 63, 105; Bibliothèque des Arts Decoratifs, Paris, Fonds Henri Le Secq, 32; Collection Bibliothèque Historique de la Ville de Paris, 35, 62; Collection Centre Canadien d'Architecture/Canadian Centre for Architecture, Montréal, 68; Collection de la Société Française de Photographie, 20, 21, 23, 25, 28, 49, 54, 61, 64, 65, 69; Frank Horvat, 130; Gilberte Brassaï, title page, 70, 71, 89; Ilse Bing, opp. title, 81; Ilse Bing/Collection Galerie Zabriskie, Paris, New York, 122; Izis Bidermanas, front jacket; Lee Miller Archives 1990, 99; Magnum Photos/H. Cartier-Bresson, 93, 128, 129; Magnum Photos/R. Capa, 104, 109; Magnum Photos/D. Stock, 144; Marc Riboud, 101; Ministère de la Culture, France/ Association Française pour la Diffusion du Patrimoine Photographique, back jacket, 6, 75, 78, 84, 85, 86, 87, 88, 90, 91, 92, 95, 96, 97; Musée Carnavalet/Giraudon, 52; Musée Nationale des Techniques, Paris, 12; Musées de la Ville de Paris/DACS . 8, 17, 30, 31, 33, 34, 36–7, 39, 45, 56, 57, 67; Museum of Modern Art, New York, Gift of Edward Steichen, 53 (plate 6 from the portfolio of 20 photographs printed and published in an edition of 100 by Berenice Abbott from the original negatives, New York, 1956, gelatin-silver print, $6^7/8 \times 9^1/16$ in); National Gallery Canada, Ottawa, 27; Nègre Family Collection, 9, 26; Rapho Agency/R. Doisneau, 112, 118, 125, 132, 133; Rapho Agency/W. Ronis, 111, 119, 120, 126; Roger Schall, 98, 116, 117; Royal Photographic Society, Bath, 24, 55, 58; William Klein, 100, 131.

INDEX

Page numbers in *italic* refer to illustrations; those in **bold** type to the photographer's biography.

ACKNOWLEDGEMENTS

I would like to express my profound gratitude to Lucy, my wife,
to whom I owe my love of Paris and whose support, guidance and extraordinary
patience never faltered during the course of the project; to Maša Arko Vogrič, my
assistant, without whose industry, efficiency and devotion this book would never
have seen the light of day; and to Selby McCreery, whose assiduous research
spared me hours of frustration in collating and verifying information.
I would like to convey my deepest thanks to
Vivien Bowler and Lesley Baxter of Little, Brown and Company
for their patience and constant encouragement, and special thanks to
Andrew Barron for his guiding vision and sensitivity towards the project. I am
also particularly grateful to the many museums and institutions who have allowed
me to reproduce their photographs in this book, especially to Sylvain Pelly of the
Société Française de Photographie; Fabienne Muddy of Magnum Photos; Debbie
Ireland of the Royal Photographic Society; Kathleen Grosset of Rapho Agency;
Mathieu Witkovsky of the Zabriskie Gallery in Paris; Françoise Reynaud and
Catherine Tambrun of the Musée Carnavalet; Sylvie Cohen, Claude Vittiglio
and Martine d'Astier at the Association Française pour la Diffusion du
Patrimoine Photographique; and Joseph Nègre.

Café de Flore
Stock 1958